THE

QUARTERLY

EDITED BY

GORDON LISH

---

*Mayhaps you thought Q 22—which number
was one number before this number—
rather too congested with the wit of our Hogan,
which person, you may have noticed, also Hoganized
Q 21—which number was not one but two numbers
before this one—though rather more moderately
than he did Q 22. Well, fine, too bad for you—
because if you start turning pages many enough
to get yourself south enough of this page,
you will find some more serious Hoganizing going on.
Hey, but this is nothing, the Hogansville that's
south of here. It's the Hoganza that's coming south,
north, east, and west of you in the number one number
up from this number that's going to—be warned,
you look at Q 24 at your peril—
Hogan you to death.*

Look, the editor's not wild about the notion—
but, heck, it's getting to be pretty late
in the century; there's no telling what
the coming deal is going to be, everybody's
got a right to a little recklessness;
this must mean, me, I've got a lot of right
to a lot of it—so how about this for
the thing? Call me if you've got a hassle
with the *Q.* I'm at 212-572-2128.
Durando will answer if I don't answer.
Only don't get snappish if it's Durando,
a caution that is a Public Safety
announcement, in case you need to know.

THE
QUARTERLY

23 / FALL 1992

VINTAGE BOOKS

A DIVISION OF RANDOM HOUSE, INC.

NEW YORK

THE QUARTERLY (ISSN: 0893-3103) IS EDITED BY GORDON LISH
AND IS PUBLISHED MARCH, JUNE, SEPTEMBER, AND DECEMBER AT
201 EAST 50TH STREET, NEW YORK, NY 10022. SUBSCRIPTION REQUESTS—
FOUR ISSUES AT $48 US, $60 CANADIAN, $54 US OVERSEAS—AND ADDRESS
CHANGES SHOULD BE SENT TO THE ATTENTION OF SUBSCRIPTION OFFICE,
22ND FLOOR. ORDERS RECEIVED BY JANUARY 31 START WITH MARCH NUMBER;
BY APRIL 30, JUNE NUMBER; BY JULY 31, SEPTEMBER NUMBER; BY OCTOBER 31,
DECEMBER NUMBER. SEE LAST PAGE FOR PURCHASE OF BACK NUMBERS.

MANAGEMENT BY ELLEN F. TORRON
COORDINATION BY GEORGE DONAHUE
DESIGN BY ANDREW ROBERTS
ART DIRECTION BY CATHRYN S. AISON AND REBECCA AIDLIN
ASSISTANCE BY NEAL DURANDO, SIV RAFFORD, BETH HARRISON,
RICK WHITAKER, AND STEVE CHO

THE QUARTERLY WELCOMES THE OPPORTUNITY TO READ WORK OF EVERY
CHARACTER, AND IS ESPECIALLY CONCERNED TO KEEP ITSELF AN OPEN FORUM.
MANUSCRIPTS MUST BE ACCOMPANIED BY THE CUSTOMARY RETURN MATERIALS,
AND SHOULD BE ADDRESSED TO THE EDITOR. THE QUARTERLY MAKES THE UTMOST
EFFORT TO OFFER ITS RESPONSE TO MANUSCRIPTS NO LATER THAN ONE WEEK
SUBSEQUENT TO RECEIPT. OPINIONS EXPRESSED HEREIN ARE NOT NECESSARILY
THOSE OF THE EDITOR OR OF THE PUBLISHER.

COVER BY CHIP KIDD

ISBN: 0-679-74224-7

GUESS WHAT. WORD IS FROM TORRON THAT WE'RE CATCHING UP ON GETTING CONTRACTS
OUT TO CONTRIBUTORS CONTEMPORANEOUSLY WITH THE ACQUISITION OF MATERIALS FOR THE
ISSUE TO WHICH THEY, THE CONTRIBUTORS, ARE CONTRIBUTING. GUESS WHAT ELSE. THIS
MEANS IT WON'T BE LONG BEFORE WE'RE UP-TO-DATE WITH FORKING OVER WHAT WE OWE
TO SAME FOR SUCH. HEY, COME ON—BE FAIR. YOU HAVE ANY IDEA OF HOW CRAZY-HARD
TORRON'S LABOR FOR THIS MAGAZINE IS? TALK ABOUT CRUSHING ROCK, DID YOU KNOW
SISTER ELLEN'S DOING IT TO GRANITE SATURDAYS AND SUNDAYS AT FOUR IN THE MORNING
ALL BY HER LONESOME IN THE GREAT BIG RANDOM HOUSE BUILDING? COME TELL US HOW
YOU'D LIKE TO BE ALL BY YOUR LONESOME COME FOUR IN THE MORNING IN A GREAT BIG
RANDOM HOUSE–STYLE BUILDING. FORTY STORYS OF IT AND JUST ONE STORY OF YOU?
HEY, LET'S FACE IT, PAL, TORRON'S GOT SAND, WHEREAS SOME OF US, IT'S NO BETTER THAN
POWDER, YOU KNOW? ANYWAY, IF WE'VE LATELY PUBLISHED YOU, THEN WE'RE FINALLY
GOING TO GET AROUND TO PAYING YOU—LATE, YES—BUT SOONER THAN YOU THINK.
ANOTHER THING IS THIS—IF YOU THINK IT'S TOUGH BEING TORRON, JUST GO AHEAD AND TRY
BEING ANDREW ROBERTS FOR JUST ONE LOUSY EDITION OF THE LOLLAPALOOZA YOU'RE RIGHT
THIS INSTANT LOOKING AT. MAN, YOU DON'T KNOW THE HALF OF IT, OKAY? P.S. TORRON
JUST WALKED IN AND SAID FOR US TO SHUT UP, THAT SHE'S ALL CAUGHT UP. DAMN.

THE QUARTERLY

23 / FALL 1992

THE QUARTERLY

When my brother and I would have to sleep in the same bed together, my brother's mouth would always be beside my ear when we were going to sleep and I would always hear him humming what to me sounded like a kind of hymn we used to have to sing in the church where we were always made to go. I could never tell if he was doing it for me—if he was humming to help me to go to sleep—or if it was for himself, if it was a way for him to put himself to sleep. Even if he ever even knew he was doing it, I could never tell, so soft it was, so deep inside his throat—like breathing.

—GEOFFREY BROWN

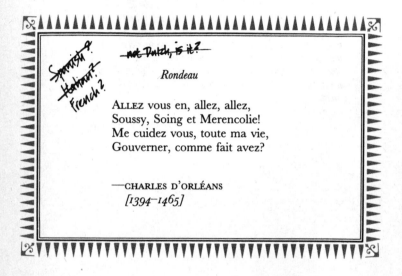

Spanish?
Italian?
French?

~~not Dutch, is it?~~

Rondeau

ALLEZ vous en, allez, allez,
Soussy, Soing et Merencolie!
Me cuidez vous, toute ma vie,
Gouverner, comme fait avez?

—CHARLES D'ORLÉANS
[1394–1465]

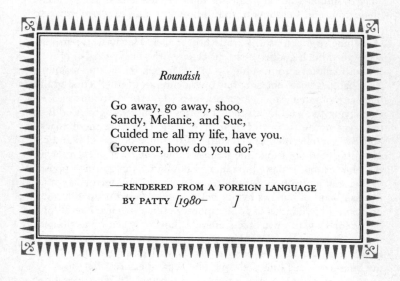

Roundish

Go away, go away, shoo,
Sandy, Melanie, and Sue,
Cuided me all my life, have you.
Governor, how do you do?

—RENDERED FROM A FOREIGN LANGUAGE
BY PATTY [1980—   ]

THE COST OF PRODUCING THESE PAGES IS MET BY INSTRUMENT OF A TWENTY-FIRST CENTURY "HANDS ACROSS THE WINE-DARK SEAS" OUTREACH PILOT GRANT (#2787-4-XX1.C) MOUNTED UNDER THE JOINT SPONSORSHIP OF THE INTER-LINGUAL UNION, THE E.J. CRACKEL PROJECT FOR WORLD MUTUALITY, AND TEEN 'N' TWENTY DRESSES OF RAHWAY, NEW JERSEY. *THE QUARTERLY* WISHES TO ACKNOWLEDGE ITS GRATITUDE TO THESE ORGANIZATIONS FOR THEIR EXPRESSION OF TRUST IN THIS PUBLICATION'S STEWARDSHIP. THANKS, TOO, TO THE TRANSLATO WHEEL CORPORATION.

Second, Harris

Mixing together an implausible combination of pagan mythography, Darwinian primalism, S&M kink, quack anthropology, and bourgeois, coffee-table Nietzscheanism, megalomaniac Camille Paglia would like us to believe that she is a painted savage who eats babies for breakfast, a walking, talking *vagina dentata*. In chaste, neoclassic prose full of statements about the "long slow suck, the murk, the ooze" of "my chthonian swamp" and limpid references to "nature spuming and frothing, its mad spermatic bubbles endlessly spilling out and smashing in that inhuman round of waste, rot, and carnage," she treats us to the lyrical excesses of a style that reminds us of nothing so much as a B-grade horror flick. Her wicked persona of a stilettoed bitch goddess, who prickteases the heavyweights of Western culture into queuing up for their turn in her one-woman gang bang, reflects not only her own delusions of intellectual grandeur but those of other American academics whose pipe dreams of electrifying the world with their theories are increasingly at odds with the unglamorous reality of their profession. The more the flunkies of postmodern officialdom have come to resemble a class of bland civil servants, the more exotic the fantasies they entertain of themselves, so that their status as petty bureaucrats now stands in glaring opposition to their self-perception as radicals, subversives, and terrorists—a freakish band of outlaws living reckless and dangerous lives in the uncivilized hinterlands of contemporary critical theory. Not all of the blame for Paglia's invincible smugness, however, can be attributed to the swaggering bravado of her assault on conventional images of the passionless scholar. The mass media themselves have contributed to the outrageous self-burlesque she obediently performs for the amusement of the American public—a spectacle of self-congratulation so appalling that it inspires a sense at once of anger and acute embarrassment, of not knowing where to look, of wanting to disperse the snickering crowd that baits this dancing bear, this innocent creature from the wilds who, worked up into a frenzy by the attention of the press, tumbles and somersaults, lurching around the ring of the big top, confused by the noise and the bright lights. In the degrading routine Paglia puts on for the benefit of docile scribes she spoon-feeds with unsubstantiated claims that she is "one of the smartest women who has ever written" and "the most important . . . intellectual since Susan Sontag," the desperation of the American academic has finally been unleashed as she storms out of the position of insignificance and marginality in which professors have been immured for generations and charges towards the bright red cape she descries in the distance, the beguiling prospect of fame the media flourish before her like matadors.

—**DH**

THE
QUARTERLY

America

There were people out there doing things. I read the newspapers. I read the magazines. I read everything. I knew what they did, always at night, when everyone was sleeping. I had prescriptions. I was a customer. I knew about what happened.

They moved around at night, in dark clothes, in dusty cars, and they brought their tools with them. Rope and handcuffs, guns and knives with tape on the handles, lengths of wire, duct tape for eyes and mouths. Some of them used hammers and pliers, sometimes just rocks or their hands.

And they didn't look strange, didn't look funny, didn't twitch or say odd things when other people were around. In Nevada and Oregon and Utah and Colorado they said he had blond hair, was friendly, was handsome, talked carefully, had a smile, had nice teeth. In California he played the guitar. In Chicago he was tall and had blue eyes. In Texas he was blond, had been a Marine, had been a marksman. He was a dapper fellow, had dark hair, could talk. A killer couldn't talk like that, could he?

I represent a modeling agency, and I'd like to talk to you, and if it's not too embarrassing—and I know how some ladies would be too shy—I'd like, if I may, to take your measurements. To keep on file at the office, for when assignments come up.

The landlord asked him to check the faucets, the radiators, the paint on the bedroom ceiling. The gas company was worried about a leak, the power company about electrical sockets, the fire department about smoke. There was a mayor's commission taking a survey for housing needs, for the benefit of the elderly. There was a survey being conducted for a nationally-known concern. People willing to participate were immediately eligible for the grand drawing, for a trip to South America, for a dinette set, for a washer and dryer, for everything.

. . .

I wore black socks and glasses to the doctor's office. I had terrible headaches. I was working too hard, wasn't able to relax, couldn't sleep very well. I had to put ice packs on my head, had to lie down in the dark, had to lie still as a blanket.

Was I allergic to anything? they asked.

They said, You have to be careful with this, and filled out the sheet on the pad. You have to avoid driving, and avoid alcohol, and be very careful not to mix them.

One was Q.I.D., one was T.I.D.

They said, Call in six months.

At home, I took two tablets. After an hour I took two more, and then two more after that. I itched. There was a strand of something, a web on my face. I brushed it away. I went downstairs to talk to my mother and father. They weren't doing much, were trying to relax. They said things were okay, but they were worried about me. About the headaches and the doctors and why I wasn't doing anything. Just painting houses and not eating enough and sleeping half the day and reading that stuff.

I said, What was it like when you were growing up?

They wanted to know why I was always asking about that.

Dad said, Now that seems truly morbid.

Dad said all the cars were black, and there was no such thing as television. Mail was delivered twice a day, and a postcard cost a penny.

There wasn't as much noise, Mom said.

I could feel the pills—six or eight or ten of them—from my toes to the hair on my head. All the way down my arms and legs.

Mom said, It was nice.

They went out at night, and they drove in a car to the neighborhoods in the hills, above the city, and down below they could see the millions of lights down there, an ocean, a sea, a lake of jewels. The houses were enormous and dark, and had high dense bushes all around them. There were smooth lawns and patios, and many houses had pools that were sky-blue and that had underwater lights on all night, and lawn furniture around the sides of the patios and pools. This was in summer, in June and July and August, and doors were unlocked, and screens were on windows, and the air was so still they could hear a car a mile away, far down in the canyon, on the road that had been built into the side of a hill. The noise seemed to come from the other side of the bushes, but it was much farther away. They knew that, knew how tricky things could be at two or three in the morning. How shadows were animals or people, and light was so faint that skin almost glowed, eyes were large and shiny, and from the lawns they were sure they could hear people breathing inside, could hear them murmur in sleep, could hear them turn over and press a hand to the side of the face. Sleeping people were so open, seemed so young, were newborns even. Just lying there, surrounded by warmth, their eyes closed, their breathing deep and regular, their minds and senses given over to dreams, to horses that flew, and to drifting trees, and to a sky the color of roses.

There were four of them one time. The three women and the tall man, and they checked the front door, and couldn't believe it.

The door was unlocked.

People were so stupid. It was amazing. Maybe because this was California, and warm all the time, was always sunny, and oranges grew in trees right outside.

Nature was kind.

The world was good.

The living room was enormous, and had beams in the ceiling, and a huge fireplace, and couches. The breathing was louder in there, and one of them, the blond woman from Iowa or Nebraska or somewhere near there, began to giggle, and he—the tall man— had to shush her, even though he knew the feeling. Oh, he wanted to laugh at how stupid they were. They had no idea at all. No clue whatsoever, in there, sleeping as if they were four years old and cowboys and movie stars and fighter pilots in the sky.

His heart was a drum in a band, was driving everything forward, and he had no idea how many of them were sleeping, through that doorway, behind other doors that probably were not even closed. But, of course, he did not know what would happen either, knew just that they—the four of them—were there, were standing next to the couches and the polished tables and the lamps that looked like balloons in the light from the moon outside.

Then the blond woman started to move, crouched over, in a sideways, sliding motion. She moved between the couches, in front of the fireplace, past the big window, past the shiny tables and bulbous lamps, and she began to hiss as she moved, hiss so softly that they wouldn't have been able to hear her, her tongue and teeth and lips, and all the esses like a pipe, like a radiator, like something in the grass, if it hadn't been so late and so utterly still. Then the other two women started moving and hissing softly, and the tall man joined them, and all four were gliding sideways, were hissing so low that it was only air, and they crouched low to the floor, to the carpet, as they moved, and any minute, any second someone might hear, might know, might sense in sleep, and might open his eyes.

If they stood up, paused at the bedroom door, peeked down the hall, toward the living room. If they came out—anyone. Someone with matted hair, with sleep-puffed eyes. Someone in a nightgown, in pajamas, in undershorts, in underwear. Someone naked, his flesh ghostly in the weird light.

What then?

The blond woman picked a glass ball off an end table. The ball was clear and had a starfish embedded in it, and she held it up—this creature from under the water and now under glass. There in the moonlight, and named for the sky.

Ssss, she said softly, and pressed the glass to her throat, to her neck, to her breast. Then she went to the front door, and all of them glided out, still crouched over, and the lawn was moonlit. Someone had plugged it in. And the pool was blue like daylight and was moving.

She giggled again. They all giggled.

. . .

I slept fourteen hours, and when I woke up my head was lead, was thick and dense and heavy, and my mouth was dry. I lit a cigarette and blew smoke at the ceiling and listened.

The house was empty. Everyone had gone to work, had gone out—and when I moved my head, it took me a second or two to catch up with the movement. There was a shadow, an echo, to everything. My lips couldn't grip the cigarette right.

The paper was on the table in the kitchen. A woman had been found Sunday by hikers in the Blue Hills Reservation. There was a sock on one foot and a thin gold chain around one wrist. There was a body found in a dumpster in Saugus. There was a dead man in the trunk of a car, in the parking lot of a bowling alley on Route One. There were young women missing. There was a spot of blood on the pillowcase.

At night, sometimes, I walked, after the first two or three cups of coffee, after the pills. I walked through the neighborhoods of Newton, the lights of the traffic streaming past, and I crossed the Massachusetts Turnpike in Newtonville, then went right off Lowell Avenue, and went up the steep streets to West Newton Hill, where the houses were enormous, and there were three or four cars in the circular driveways, where there was sculpture on some of the lawns. At dusk, at dinner time, the windows were orange and yellow, and the people inside, as they stood at the kitchen counters and sinks, as they sat on the couches and rocking chairs in dens and living rooms, seemed handsome and calm and infinitely assured. They wore eyeglasses, and had beautiful graying hair. They were thin, and the collars of their shirts were starched, and they had heavy gold or silver watches on their wrists.

When it was dusk, when it was six or seven in the evening in October or March, and mostly dark, I walked down driveways and sat on swings in backyards, sat on benches that had been set under oak or elm or maple trees. I watched the lighted windows, and saw the people, and heard traffic, and saw airplanes winking across the night sky. I took more pills from my watch pocket, swallowed them, then stood up and cut through the bushes or climbed a fence into another backyard.

He had blinding headaches, headaches that were so powerful they made tears run down his face. He typed a note. He wrote: I don't quite understand what is compelling me to type this note. I have been to a psychiatrist. I have been having fears and violent impulses. I've had some tremendous headaches in the past. I am prepared to die. After my death I wish an autopsy be performed on me to see if there's any mental disorder.

His wife's name was Kathy.

He wrote, I've decided to kill Kathy tonight. I love her very much. I don't want her to have to face the embarrassment my actions will surely cause her.

He went to his mother's apartment and killed her. He wrote, I love my mother with all my heart.

He wrote, 12:00 A.M.—Mother already dead. Three o'clock—both dead.

He wrote, This is my answer.

He went to the observation deck of the tower with two pistols and a 35-millimeter Remington rifle and began to shoot. He shot forty-six people and killed sixteen.

He was blond, had blue eyes.

In Chicago, in Boston, and in Houston and Seattle, he walked quietly, walked quickly, walked with his arm in a sling, or used crutches, or seemed to have trouble carrying his books. He dropped them, and a young woman outside the library helped him pick them up, and he thanked her, said she was very kind, was very thoughtful, very pretty too, if she didn't mind his saying so.

Sometimes he had a black wallet with a badge pinned to it, and he had handcuffs too. He went to bus stations, and coffee shops that were open all night, where there were women nearby, under streetlights, in doorways, in front of stores.

They said to him, Where are you from? And the kid with dark eyes said, Baton Rouge, sir, and spoke softly, shyly, with a trace of a drawl, a trace of the South.

He was fifteen, had left home, had left the old bastard in December, just before Christmas, and didn't think the old man even knew he was gone.

C'mon, they said, and the kid thought of a room with a bed, and a dresser at the foot of the bed, and a peephole in the door. Green paint. Baloney sandwiches for lunch and dinner, the soup, the kid two doors down with the tattoo on the back of his hand. The one in the shower with the soap, saying, Hey, hey. His hand full of soap. You. I mean you.

My grandmother said the things people would say just to get in the newspapers, just to get on television, and how people were supposed to believe about the grapefruit and the tissues. And that thing in Philadelphia, that hotel. All those Legionnaires dying, all those long, carpeted halls, the doors to rooms, the guys downstairs in the dining rooms and bars. Big guys with stomachs sagging over their belts, with red faces, with watery eyes. Cigars and cigarettes and stories. In Georgia, they'd say. In Germany or Paris or coastal England. In the Pacific, where the sky was so blue you needed sunglasses, where the water was infinite like the heavens.

And then at night, in their rooms, the pain in their bowels was extraordinary, was as powerful as disease, and that cold shaky feeling all over. Like the flu.

The blue tablets made everything slow. They didn't make things as loose as the white ones. But they were good in between.

At two A.M. I could blink, and say things softly, lying on the bed in my room. Say things out loud, but quiet as a pillow.

Hey, I said.

Hey.

Hey.

And I could almost see sound waves leave my mouth and rise to the flat gray ceiling, and the candle flickered, and the waves of sound reached the ceiling and rippled like a pebble into water, and lapped and lapped for a long time.

Someone in Missouri had disappeared, had been walking home from school, had never reached home.

In a town of less than two thousand.

Come to me.

Come inside to me, and there was music that was so beautiful and so sweet that no one could keep from listening.

In June, on Gainsborough Street, on Commonwealth Avenue, in Lynn, north of Boston, on Grove Street, on Columbia Road, on Huntington Avenue, in Salem, in Lawrence, in Vermont, in Virginia, somewhere north of Atlanta, out there at night, moving in the air. As soft as sleep, in their heads, sleeping in Missouri, in Massachusetts, in California, or in Houston or Seattle. Under streetlights. In a movie, in a dream. **Q**

The National Terminal Show

Remember. Until the lights come on, there is no use arranging for anyone else to come down. Fly in early and go straight to the Center. Look for Manny. Stop worrying—on the first day, they are all Manny. Say something like: "Remember me? Last spring—D.C." Shake hands the way he expects, a little tentative. Sometimes it works. Sometimes he believes he remembers.

"Oh, sure, I remember you, Angel," Manny will say. "You bring us lunch from outside."

At this stage, it will be cold and gray at the Center, just a hint of solar filtering in from somewhere unfathomable. You will hear beings on the darker levels overhead, their distinctive calling: What now?

"Manny." Say it like that, as if he were Tom Bloody Someone. "I have a little bit of a problem." As if we needed something only he could provide. Which is no lie at the moment. "Manny, I ordered power yesterday."

"Did you test your spot, Angel?"

"Manny, it's dead as . . ." Stop—don't waste time searching for similes—just get to the matter. "Come over to East Wing, Manny, will you? I mean, the source is there. You can see the source, hanging down from Three Level. But it is not connected to my plug. To my neighbor's, to Proto-Solutions, yes, but it's not coming down to me. And I want it, Manny—I want it yesterday." Move closer to this man with the power. For a second, he will become unique, a condition that can only make him happy and very uncomfortable at the same time.

"Okay," he'll say, backing away a little. We guarantee this part. "Your section is not my section, but I will get you a crew. I will get one for you ASAP."

"Not ASAP, Manny. Yesterday."

"Hey. Angel. Do not ask for miracles."

Watch him pocket the tip.

Learn to expect chaos. *Absolutment* howling, formless chaos. Learn to expect piles of machinery and rubbish from the last show still crowding the entries, obstructing progress. Mohammed's mountain, whether it is ours or someone else's obsolescent mess.

Now gain access to the staging area, where monstrous vehicles, spouting monoxides, reverse gears scraping, snoggle up to the docks. All over the Center, industry is trashing the entire system—rushing in all-new updated hardware of more durable design, accessing and receiving software, pulse after pulse of it invisibly arriving on waves of air.

Now. Check off every one of our components as it comes through. Be sure each module is marked with the proper logo. Otherwise, no telling where it will end up.

Then soon, very soon, get a line out to home office, and this time do not take no. "Billy Graves." Just tell them no. "No substitutes. I do not want to be, one hour before opening, with a software man when what I have is a hardware problem. I like a man who can handle a board as well as a bug, a soldering iron *and* a Sys-Gen."

Remember, we are not technical. We are display. We are not supposed to sweat the small stuff.

"I don't care whose base is down." Go on. "I don't care if it's the King of Jordan's." Yes, we can talk that way right now. We are pretty irreplaceable right now. Remember who stayed when the whole firm was going under, ready to sink with the first delinquent note. Remember years before that, right after schooldays, when the machine was only a dream in the old man's garage in Palo Alto. Remember who passed up the offer-of-the-year from Proto-Solutions, just because the old man said please, do not do this to me. Way before the son took over.

"Hey, I don't care if Billy Graves is on the moon. This is National Terminal time—I want him down here yesterday." All right, say it. Say please.

Hold until they give out Billy's flight number. Then take old

Manny a plain coffee with something in it, and by midnight, there will be power. Good. Tomorrow, the silk goes up. First thing.

Billy should not understand what he is. He should not realize how valuable he has become. There is no one in the West who can wire up the alpha prototype and simulate simultaneous functions like Billy Graves. At least, no one we have employed. But we need him a little shaky.

So next morning, at LAX, at Arrivals, make him place the announcement at the Infodesk. Let him search. Watch him across Baggage for a full minute before the turn, the acknowledgment. Shake his hand or do not.

Just think. In the time it takes Billy to settle every tool he might ever need into the trunk of our rental Lincoln, the silk will be almost up. Canopy work is union, so we cannot touch it, can't even turn the crank. Park the car in the Exhibitors' lot, while blue silk slowly rises, suspended on invisible wires, corporate colors dividing the display and everyone who walks into the display from the tangled workings above.

Relax. You have the best technical support on the floor, the most appealing. He asks a lot of questions, and everyone likes that. Within an hour, Billy Graves will assemble a set-up crew of men and women who are genuinely happy to be working, without knowing why. Crates will soon spill their heavy components onto the thick carpet delineating our space. Soon Billy is singing, "What now?" just like everyone else, even though he knows exactly what is now. He has done his homework; he has read the National Terminal Show manual on the plane; and yesterday, he has shared a six-pack with Quality Control. If there were creepers discovered right before the ship date last month, too late to modify, Billy is aware. Count on it.

Concentrate on the big picture. Leave the Center and go out into the surrounding accommodations. Find out where everyone is that we might ever need to connect with. Who is hiring? Who is de-employing? Hit every hospitality suite at the Atrium Level. Scout the competition. (Hint: Who has hot hors d'oeuvres?) Only hold a drink. Talk Ruggedized. Talk HERB protection. Visit the hair-and-face place and get fixed. Have an après-dinner cocktail with command and then with control. Establish press ops for the son, who will be down mid-show maybe.

On opening day, take Billy to breakfast in the Center cafe. Check his checklist. Ask him how he slept. Tell him we do not know what we would do without him. At the moment, not a total lie, with the son arriving maybe.

Eat something, anything.

Three hours before the doors open, orient our sales staff as they arrive. Present our personnel with work schedules, position them at strategic corners, provide them the latest spiel—"Certain electronic functions must stay up, even if personnel do not survive specifically." Ask them to practice saying this three times very fast. Talk strategy. Talk tactics. Tell each salesperson the same joke.

Two hours before the doors open, walk the floors. Visit the others, familiar faces and bodies and machines from past product launches. Discuss the market. Discuss prevailing currents.

One hour before the doors open, look at the new prototype and say something to Billy like: "The color's wrong. Everything except the silk should appear grayer, more ruggedized."

Say to Billy, "See, Billy, as soon as anyone walks under the silk, everything about us should say Heat, Explosion, Radiation, and Blast-protection. Eternalware."

Say to Billy, "Fix it."

If the bell chimes, log on. Maybe Mom is saying via modem, "The CEO is coming soon." Maybe Mom is typing, "Yes. I am sure. I just made the arrangements, and he is flying down on Day 6, and the color better be right."

Well, what then? Say to Billy, "Fix it. Please."

Stand between the freshly-painted machine and all bodies. The aisles, by this time, will teem and echo with executives coupled with processing managers, purchasing officers, and vacationing spouses. One hundred men in tuxedos have been hired to behave as robots dressed as men. Two hundred women in sequined gowns have been hired to walk the white mezzanines, reciting input-output ratios through concealed remote microphones. A man concealed within a Plexiglas robot on wheels has been hired to flirt indiscriminately.

This is the easy part. Simply stay in position, keeping the clients happy and well-informed. Say things both intelligent and inane. All of a sudden at noon on the fifth day, while eating a hot dog at a stand-up counter next to the editor of *Federal Electronics Times,* decide to ask our Vice President for New Product Marketing for a step up. Decide to ask him this at the first available window. Or, if not that, buy something very dear very soon.

All this time, Billy is disappearing for hours, then appearing moments before a demo crash. How does he know? But believe. He will not let us down.

And if, in the middle of the night, Billy arises and walks into a wall, maybe he has simply forgotten where he is. Coming back to bed, he might ask, "So what happened?"

"What?"

"Between you and your husband?"

Say something to Billy like, "Nothing happened."

Go ahead and order the limo. Who knows? Maybe the son will simply arrive, look in, and then leave it to us again. Or maybe he will give a press conference. In any case, the limo will be ready. Maybe he'll want to cruise the bars of Long Beach with a Welsh joint-venture man, then up as far as West Hollywood, by this time not knowing why he invited the two Australian female security guards or how the Arabian couple got in the limo at all. Or maybe there has been some mistake--they are only a Mediterranean couple—but no one in the vehicle is certain.

Spend the evening buying drinks for everyone the CEO points to. Everyone except the robot. He has been paid enough already. Settle into a corner booth with the joint-venture man from Wales, watching beings on several stages impersonating Tina or Marilyn. Listen to the man from Wales recite the Western World's longest words. After a certain space of time, everything sounds like the hymns of childhood. Everything begins to rhyme. Remember your purse at each point. Spend three thousand dollars.

Then, what if it is late morning on closing day, and the CEO decides he likes the new shade of gray? Maybe he says this to the Vice President for New Product Marketing as they wave good-bye and walk down the tube onto the flight. Suddenly, he may seem so much like his father, it will be almost unbelievable. For a moment, there may be a feeling, like being extremely satisfied or extremely tired.

Return to the Center. Next, okay, what if Billy says something like, "I quit."? Just a for-instance. He has had a better offer. What then?

One option. Walk out—leave the tear-down boys to Billy. Billy would not simply desert the project before it is over. Billy is too good. Have faith. Anyway, it's in his contract: every module into its proper crate, then off to the next show. Six more sites and we loop back to the valley.

Cruise over to Accommodations and rest.

Call the children. **Q**

Evening of the Yarp

Darn, it were boring. Wisht I were a hawk or crab. When I seen him first, I leapt out of my face for glad cause nothing moving lately. But only rabbit nibble and run headfirst into the bottom of the purple cane. Deacon Charles at the VT school say go ahead and write like this dont change. He wants to see it quick cause I seen the Yarp. Or somebody like him. Xcuse me, please, for not correct, but I am hard attempting to spell at least sweller it being so important. Of a mountain man nineteen first that day at two forty-one o'clock afternoon on the watch I found at the road going up to Mrs. Skatt's house.

The sin of the old people, I wondert what it was, cause I dint feel it. The evil things of Roonswent Dover, which is me, werent felt by me like the others cause I had no feltedness of their kind of sin. I found out the Yarp dint too.

He was a man hitchhiking where dont nobody come ever up a red ditch juncted to a road so dirty and spit out red on the paving. He was a true-looking lean man near hungery looking in a high collar white city shirt but no necktie up on it. I passed him, then slapped my thigh. Why not? I'm so miserable bored. Maybe this man knewn something markable or a good thing to seek. Him wanting a ride up that ditch where nobody but old woman Skatt lives. Rained down to gullies, that road. But we figure she be so hungery she walk out of there, down the mountain with her crooked feet, buffalo toenails, and ruint smell. I backed up and he looked in the window. I say cant you see no truck nor even tractor could get up that gullied red road? He said he would go on with me and rest and see Missus Skatt later. He sat down. No suitcase, bag, nor cane, nor hat—just coming out of winter and going to near freeze this night. Thanks for the lift. You know where you are? I asted him. Yes, I been here plenty time and I know your

Missus Skatt very, very well. It dont matter much when I get there. Sooner or later. But I will go with you to the store.

I asted him how he knewn I was going to the store (and I was). He said I had the look of a store visit on me. Nobody much confused him, and now he was hungery, feeling low and getting chill. He gave me a cigar for my trouble and said it was the kind governors and rulers smoked from Latin America. We lit up and I was feeling chumly. He asted me would there be music at the store. This struck me goofy. Of course there were a radio at ever store and a televisioner too. And would there be food? I turned over to him saying what else would there be a store to be a store at all, certain it has food, gas, oil, shells, bait, sardines, herrings, rat cheese, and two old geezer at a wood stove playing Risk and playing Macky Vellens. He said what. I repeated. He pronounced it better. The writer of the *Prince* they use as a handbook to Risk, taking on personalities, book falling depart apieces through the generations. Mr. Simpson and Gene James owned it with they smart goat that makes change. I swear.

Then that man, the Yarp, he said shut up. Riding aside me afortunate my charity, he said shut up ragely. It were glum. I werent happy. But couldnt get mad cause he seem a danger now. I dont want to hear none of your tales, boy, he kept on it, too many tales come out of these mountains and everwhere. There shouldnt be any tales.

I said well you can see the goat with his front foot.

But he hissed or spat.

So I look out the window away from him. Stopt talk.

In your mind you thinking you paying for the gas and tires hauling me.

And it was true, what he said.

We had eleven mile to go. It was crooked high down to low, then high again. Not even a dead dog nor cat nor chicken keep you company under the overhangs of them sweaty rocks. I aint nere liked them and now, getting on dark. The mountains, I feel they live and squeeze in on you to a narrow lane when nobody around. I nere give up that feeling sinct I was a kid. It aint

Arkansas or no real place. Now come sleet, specking my poor dusty glass all acracked. Which I didnt like, what with the sun running down either.

We'll have a nice snow tonight, the Yarp adventured.

The quiet I was keeping dint make no call to break it. So I remaint quiet. Nineteen or not, I was frighted. But if the quiet woulder asked me, I woulder said you fool, its on too late to snow, that sleet is just a peck from some froze cloud way up there. It April, you fool.

Yes, itll catch Missus Skatt just unfreezing from the winter. She wont have enough wood. Im sure glad Im going with you to the warm store, Roonswent Dover.

Yes, he called my name. There aint no way of knowing my name and be a stranger. Cause I go by Bill Dover to everbody knowlege. I aint got even no license plate on this truck. You can see ten mile clear out here. Cant be no stranger as ever came near your house, nor your daddy or mommer, that you dont know about. Our part of the county cant have no stranger moren ten minute. So it were cold quiet now, believe it, no heater in my truck, only a lantern in case of a mountain accident. Lucky if they matches in that glove apartment. I couldnt get no speed outer her neither and we aint got to the real high passes yet. We was in a holler and then a vale, pinking out to the sides. There was some sun a bit so sudden I got brave.

But you shunt know my name.

He nored me.

You know too many legends, boy. Everbody does. You got to lie to stay halfway interested in yourself, dont you? The imagination is what wrecks it. They shouldnt never imagined heaven nor hell. They shoulder taken their years, thats all. You already know the more you think of something aforehand it isnt anything like that at all. They be legending, though. They be doing wrong and doing nothing, bargaining with heaven or hell. They shoulder just taken their years and practiced being dumb. Already that school is confusing you and hurting your mind, Roonswent Dover, son of Grady and Miriam.

I just fix small engines, I aventured.

You lie!

That last shout was good for another two mile of silents.

It snows here when there aint no snows anywhere else near. We must be higher, higher than all Arkansas and Missouri. In our county the Indian were never pushed out and we has whole fullblood Indians. But they are innocent. All the killing and stealing on tourists or policemen or sometimes a local for peculiar reasons is done not by them. Some said it were womens—womens and girls. A Indian told me that. Now our Indians are Nini Indians. They fought on the Souths side and had slaves where nare white man here fought for either side, most for not knowing there were a war on and the rest, said my Uncle Rell, because they were drunk or idiots. A Ozark army might have swayed the war, says Rell. Our family wernt interbred. But some, come to church and school too, theyr daughters get pregnant by them or theyr sons. So the Indian were defeated, and without slaves they moved up here from like Paragould near the river and sorrowed-out and become puny. Anybody can whip a Indian a head taller than him. A girl could do it. It is still a agony how many years, a thousand years after the war, the Indian is in deep sorrow even to plant a bean or tote water or feed his dog. They groan out loud all the time, feeble. And they hates it, cursing Robert E. Lee, who promised them slaves all the future. So theyr homes is tragic, likely to be a stricken old bus or a natural cave or sometimes what I saw, they tooken to living secret under a white man house that they dug a hole under it. And they are in ever abandoned shack or outhouse. They are in so fast. They might be puny, but they are quick. Whole families can get on a squat quicker than deer fleas. The old shacks and cabins here and there was left over from the diamond rush when my pa was a boy. Reason Im explaining the Indian is they had legends more than us. Theyr chief drives a schoolbus to the VT school and will lie like a mockingbird back and forth to it. The bus dont allow nare radio. So that Indian, Don Suchi Nini, sing to us these stories and believes he is the one who will change them back to real. They still want slaves. Don Nini say the whites better stay strong or, clunk, they be Indian slave come nigh. When I was littler, he had me making my grades. I went to the VT so I wouldnt be no slave. We know what theyr thinking, and theyr everwhere, slunking round and creeping lenthwise in some Ozark ledge or listening from some nookery. You cant do nothing about it. Xcept sometime a girl will kill one, and they are set back in theyr revolution for a few week. I never treated nare Indian bad. Most here dont. They might be puny, but they scare me. The men dont care whether they got on a dress or overall. They melt right in front of you into a line of trees. Three mile up from the store on that last bad mountain, this Indian goes across my lights, which, wouldnt you know, full of snow, but he was old and naked except for wading boots. It just made me shake. I never seen nare like it, cracking my teeth that way. Then there were a little mountain girl coming after him with a fork hoe. What a dreadsome ancient sneer on her face. They come off the side of the mountain across the road and maintained on down the mountain where nothing but no goat should get a perch—on down to awful black night rock near the pitch of a well.

Oh! I said out. You see that? Hands bout to tear off the steering wheel.

I didnt see anything at all, lad, said him.

Everthing since he got in that truck was mocking me, minding back. Xcept maybe that speech on legends, hell, and heaven.

The snow was churning and up in the road, some storm blowing down about three mile high, from the North Pole, only in our county. But it was I knewn he was the Yarp in a way already, I bet. He was lost over there in the dark seat. Maybe he dint see that old Indian and girl. Wouldnt you know the engine quit and overheat and I had to coast down? Ive did it before, all the way to the store. Xcept the unsound got to me, in the curves and sliding on them circular threads that does as tires. The quiet was outside and inside and my poor lights was flickering. I knewn Id have already been down twict and back if the Yarp wadnt with me.

You hear about murdering thieving females in these parts, said the Yarp.

I werent going to adventure. Nat Hidey, no I werent. Was peering in the snow, which it was heavier than normal snow and was gray, not white. A Yarps eyes of course is suppose to be hot yellow and his skin disappeared from his throat his voice box out so you hanging down to the ground like a slug snail, presiding on you specially when they are in groups nearby you, glooming at you, wanting something you cant give but they have to stay after it. That feebletude and they putting hands on you, that belongs more in your nightmares than a strong evil man. It gets your back clammier, your heart miserabler.

I coasted on down not talking at all like Im talking now, lights flickering at the snow that were like gray scales. Yeah, I finally got it, like fish scales, aflapping on the glass. I wouldnt look but he started shaking with cold, I guess, commenced to knocking on the tin floorboard of my Ford, gruesomish. There hadnt been lights left nor right the whole trip, nare cabin nor goodly shack even. If there were a light to commit, you hadnt sawn it.

Hurry, lad, the store, said him.

I was cold to the bones too. When, what you know, the engine caught on for maybe cooling down gainst the snow. This thing get a hundred mile on a gallon of water when its good.

Will there be music, he asted again.

Even if the radio broke, they have a televisioner that pull in a music channel all snowy. Out here for the mountains we cant barely get waves. But there is people moving, dancing in the speckled screen. We dont know the source. But there be a tiny music at it. The people is sad-looking themselves. When the music goes out entire, you just having loud snow and forms pitching and pulling at each other. But I didnt say this to the creature I knewn certain were a Yarp, chatting and shifting with cold. I wont it were light enough can see its tongue long in it and tonsils and open voice box. It makes you sick. I werent going to look over there at all. I werent getting it yet, but the Yarps smell of course would be a combination of bull spunk and road kill. Your Yarp suppose to have tiny long bird legs and big long feet too. But a Yarp doesnt have to be none of that unless the time come on him. A Yarp has

passed for a preacher! You know that? He dont know any breed.
He can be a Indian or Kentuckian or live far off in a hospital. But
he denominates in black garments. Sudden he will lift his coat and
you can see all his digestion, everthing hes eat all chewed and
gravyed-up in them tubes and holds and glands. It make you
sicker. Thered be a babys foot. Or one woman saw his stomach
and there were a human brain!

You can picture me a hard looker through that windshield.

A Yarp is weak and quick like a Indian in the legs. Thin, but
in the upper body powerful. So this thing throw through the woods
and running water and treelopes top-sided. It can reach up with
its arm and yank you down. But it aint hardly nothing underneath
but coot legs and wading feet. My grandpa knewn a family of
Yarps, peaceable, but nare eye has set on a whole family sinct his
time, which were eighty year ago, when the Ozark was founded.
A Yarp really belong in Europe or Asia is what my grandpa say.
A Yarp dont like it here in Arkansas. But some fell off accidental
in the boats going out and there we are, they come aYarping with
Vikes and Pilgrims, they dont know no breed. Like the Indian,
they would be not so scarey if they was strong and upright. They
is twict the fear to me weak and slimy, to see his feet and legs so
thin out the side low of my eyeball.

If there isnt music, lad, we must ride on, said he.

Oh, no, we dont, said I to me.

He knewn already that at the VT school we gathered with
Deacon Charles, some nine of us young hillbillies at the head of
the willow creek back of the schoolbus, the Indian chief Don Nini
with us too, listening and saying and ahearkening, at lunch.
Seemed it was, wouldnt you know, the subject of females and some
studying the old stories and some about the at-large way of the
world. Some of them had Satan with a fiddle, why Im assaying off
again here, the music. He was known to come to a dance out of
nowhere and negotiate his fiddle to warp womens and girls. But
Deacon, who is reasonable in the head and forty-five and run the
small engine course, said that was made up by jealous male hillbillies whose wives and sweethearts was taken off by a musical stran-

ger. Any slicker could do her, even out of a flat Arkansas town. You might as well say that Satan had a good car or money, which would work better. Deacon knewn the flat delta as well as us in the hills and of course was in the arm service when we was fighting, I believe, India. He said there werent even half the real tales never that they claim. Like youd think a standard Ozark person was going round hardly nothing but a blabbering tale, tales piling up in ever holler and cove. No! And a lots were did pure for government men and university people who wouldnt leave them alone and specially during the Deep Ression. In the Deep Ression times, folks often told a tale get the government interested in you as interesting, as workable, or feedable, or sometimes even traversing to you free money, which they awarded you for not coming off the mountain and mixing in nare cities, which already had too many folks. Some had went to California and messed it up terrible. The governor of California had began a new state and he didnt want no hillbillies on it. In California, they have science that grow eggs on a tree, and them hillbillies so sloppy and shuffling, they dont know how to harvest them down and walk without cracking them with their stupid damn Arkansas feet. Deacon Charles would hold up his banana at lunch and say whats this? A banana. Well, more than that, friends—youre looking at California, where I shipped out to the East. You say I went west to get East, how? Well, friends, there is a line in the ocean all stormy where everthing gets backwards, that's how! They worship whats little, like a stick. Back to the tales, he said when you then dropped the ones said by parents to scare theyr young into formity, you hadnt hardly no real tales left. No, your witches and your haints, there wasnt many of them, and the tales told about them got them wrong, my hillbilly geese, all gaggle an tongue. Your active supernaturals aint ever going to get that apparent, for one thing. He live on the rim of things and dont want to be discovered. I seen exactly one Yarp—and I been searching all my life.

Finally the store.

But it looked dim in that rain of snow. A quarter the light usually come out of there from Mr. Simpson and old Gene James, tall and gray-bald with a bowtie like some girl stood him up sixty years ago. The thing, the Yarp, hopped out, and went on in— while I gassed up and watered the truck. Ice and snow was already thick and made my truck ghosted. Oh, it were freezing. I trembled scared both, not wanting in the store but too cold not to.

The Yarp was over next to the wood stove, where they was sitting just staring at the Risk board, no pieces on it. Something was wrong. I were glad there was somebody else to share the Yarp with, even only young like I am.

He had said something made them stop and frown, Mr. Simpson out of a old blanket over him and the smart goat next to the leg of the Yarp. That goat could make change for a dollar. Signalled with his foot.

Theyr not believing I am Missus Skatts man, Roonswent, said the Yarp.

Mr. Simpson had a face long like a mules, with magnifying glasses he wore, making his eyes huge and swimming at you. He said that old woman crooked and near eighty and dyes her hair red? She on them inclines like a crab been skint. Aint no young man like you be courting her. Why youd be too young for her, son.

Before this night is over I will be with her. I have seen her many many time. I have been with her many many time.

Gene James spoke, God made the vaginer of even a plain woman so sweet that even after knucular war and it was the only thing left, the race would be continued. But she cross the line.

How could you get up there? said Mr. Simpson.

You cant hardly get up there on a hard summer day, said Gene James.

Hed of been the right age if nare man would court her, which, it made you sick to think about.

Its froze in, on top of being naught but gullies, said James.

Why, Ill walk right up there from here, said the Yarp.

Some dimwits was released on the county about when I was ten from a buswreck down a iced incline, them that wasnt killed outright. They come from the hatch in Little Rock to spy the

Ozarks. Folks liked some of them, and took them in—and some of them bred, we all knewn. Gene James looked at him and then me like he might be one, this Yarp, just now showing up from torment. You couldnt tell them from normal. But I was busy looking at that mans legs and feets. The feets were long and wide, all right—in, Ill be hung, gray scuffed brogans like an normous baby shoe. You never seen that brand nigh nowhere round here. I liked being clost to my home, three mile on.

Mr. Simpson, he would wear a gown or womens pedal-pushers, and highheel canvas sandals with bush socks, anything. So he wasnt one to pass judgment. But I was flickering with my eyes at old James, wanting him to see the infant boots. Before he could, two Ninis came in, stomping snow off. They had on blankets and towels and you couldnt tell man or woman or two of the same. Mr. Simpson spoke some Nini because he traded with them. One had on a beanie thing on its head with a rubber band under its chin, and it said something. So Mr. Simpson pointed, and the two went back and sat on the one piano bench, and the one in the beanie commenct playing the piano, Indian or bad, which was good for seventy-one out of eighty-eight keys. They took up some time from the Yarp question. You thought about the only one ever truly play that thing was away high and rich maybe on Mars by now, Len Simpson. The Yarp was closing his eyes like sweet music was alooning. I was trying to whisper *Yarp* to old James before that thing raised up his coat and made the geezer vomit and die. Gene James was a stubborn born liar. But I was the first to see the Yarp. Now someways out of my fear with four other rightly human persons, I thought I had evened with Deacon Charles. I had a true tale and would be the center of the lunch talkings for a long time. Gene James was only fifth or eighth on what hed seen true, at eighty or more.

The Yarp spoken again.

Ive a great hard long love for Missus Skatt. Shes not always what she looks to you, a goat or crab scuttling down that hill of false diamonds from her house. That is a good house, built better than most in the county. And I dont look like this all the time either. Her children is what I love, the young ones. She cooks a sumptuous venison and hare, and has a wheat patch, crushes her own meal herself for larripan bread. We have roasting ears and sweet potatoes right out of the wood ash. Im going to feed myself here.

Before no man could commence his tongue, he had come back with a bottle of herrings and sour cream, which he put upon a saltine and sucked in, not a crumb off his palm.

Missus Skatt can lasso a deer. But its her children most I love.

She never had no children. Married but barren or maybe too foul to touch, said Mr. Simpson.

She lasso them hares too, ho? said Gene James.

She stares at them till theyr hearts break, said the Yarp. That fine house was built by her husband Andrew and shortly he fell dead.

We know all that, the two geezer spoken together.

But you know only a mite, the Yarp said. Im going to tell you of her children and her charming history, which will explain why you are sitting here poor, ignorant, and stupid—with bad backs. For Missus Skatt, she run a sort of charm school, you would call it, in a town. Unknown to you, she has raised every woman in this county. And before her, another woman kin to her. While the Indian play that music I love, they cant understand me—and even when they stop, theyll just look at a mouth moving.

That one without a hat understands American, said Mr. Simpson, eyes swole in the magnifying glasses.

But that Indian wont hear a thing. This aint Indian business, said the Yarp.

Then he told a long weirded thing such as I cant hope to repeat only relying on my memory with my simular attempt.

He say all the girl children is drawn to Missus Skatt and sneaks over to her. They cant help it. When theyr ten or like that. This was even before the founding of the Ozarks with another woman. Why, even right then a girl was hauling wood to her cause she knewn it was cold and she was near out of fuel. All around the girl and the womens learnt at her knee these things—how to pleasure a man, how to coy on him, how to get inside him like a mindful tapeworm. Because she anointed them with special powerful sexual parts and strong soft arms and eary soothing voices. She coached them when to begin apleading for all they want within the county because they could never go outside the county ever and their men couldnt neither. And how to nag and harangue and beat down and whup their men, not raising a little finger. And how to make him worm small and stuck to his spot. You take mind, the Yarp said, that this county aint forever had nothing but tired sorry men droven down like a stake to their patches. They never went off to fight a war even when the whole world needed them to fight evil. Nor none of them was athletes nor only feckless at lumbering or even executing in a automobile. And none ventured out or away and couldnt hardly catch a fish on a spring day with trouts leaping on the bank. Nor with cow nor horse nor goat (the Yarp kicked the goat, and I could see Mr. Simpson and Gene James seen them whitish baby shoes of a sudden) of any count. That they died not only before theyr womens but passed over like sissies mewling and pouting ten year afore they ever hit dirt. You notice how they are coming down level and under the Indians? The Yarp pointed over at the back of that Indian who was playing, and sudden he began playing something ghostly like what were wrote by a man with a long beard in a Asian castle and sung by his beautiful daughter.

You notice too the crimes of murder and theft in the nights— all them, I tell you now, by her womens and girls. Not found by sheriffs nor nobody cause the innocence is what she drilled into them. Right now she is teaching that little wood-hauling girl how to be quick and steal, you bet. Its a thieves university, the womens. Yes, your wives too and your children-seeming girls has done it with bloody hand and prestidigitation of the fingers. They off with stolen goods, what theyr men dont get them. And sometimes they drop things, like the watch Roonswent Dover found.

He turned around. His eyes was yellow on me. I couldnt look. But down at his knees I see them chickeny legs cutting out under his black pant. I just gulped, and he was around, said Now this!

And pushed himself right up to Gene James, pulled his coat out.

Old Man James took a gander and begun vomiting, and then he fell off his chair dead with a whitened head. I was holding my hand over my eyes and didnt know what he was after for a long minute. Mr. Simpson, hed seen—but he survived, and got up and yelled to them Indian for help. But they never even turnt around.

Yes, her time has come, the Yarp said. Its over for her now. One last night of pleasure and it will be done. This Im getting xactly, I think. You wont tell none of it, Simpson, cause theyll think youve passed to senile and take away your store.

He turned to me. I was some feet off. The goat was nuzzling at my legs for comfort and baaing.

The Yarp said, if you tell anybody this, you will die, Roonswent. You are going to know whats wrong around here. But you can do nothing about it. This is your eternal curse. Which is like that of many a men. But I wont have to worry. You think you are being so kind to your mommer, taking her a fixed sewing machine. But when she takes it, you look deep like youve never looked, youll see what is there.

So Im up the hills and mounts, so give me this, said the Yarp.

He took a fold-in plastic fishing pole off the wall. It made a stout cane. He went for the door, red spots on the floor off his infant shoes.

Said he, theyll be out tonight. But just your littler girls. Even I have to swat them off. Youd think not, but I tell you, even Ive been womaned. I aint half the Yarp (he said it!) I used to be. Be a time the Indian swarm me down and break these old white bones. Yet I would die before being no slave.

He went out to the porch into the cold snow, turned for the mountains wed just came from. Them dripping smears of red was trailed out in the snow. But he dint take all that smell with him.

Mr. Simpson looked horrible miserable.

What did he show you? I asted him.

Miz Skatt's head, cooking and hollering in his belly.

The old man had dropped off his blanket and were in a ballroom gown, trembling all over his bare shoulders.

Three days later, myself and Deacon Charles and Chief Nini clambered up to Mrs. Skatts house and stood at her open heart-broke-looking door. Something were running inside. I mean cranked up. A noise. We went for it, talking loud. In the rooms, you wouldnt believe it, was piles of necklaces, tourist luggage, thermoses, deputies badges, ribbons, dresses, Nini rugs and shoes, noculars, snacks. The sound come off the screen of Mr. Simpsons missing televisioner. And there was them music people groping without no sound. Miz Skatt was laid out naked on her bed, with a old womans head and a young womans body, luptuous.

We cravened away.

So now you heared it all.

I have wrote this, not said it, hoping it will make a difference. But I dont think it will.

Im got.

Im doomed.

But Im giving it to Deacon Charles so he can send it to the governor. So give me my minutes. Stand wide. **Q**

Sayler Mans Blueds

JANDUWARY 23

De mosk awfuldest feelding haunks me. Az I'se wuz padking mi skea badg, gedding redski ta shipks yout nexd wekes, I'se suddenklees yad a viskin yov meskelf rappded insk chanes yand droppking tru da mursky wadder, depe yinto Dabee Jones lodcker. It was reel enufsks ta makes mi swet buldets. Dit was, fur lacks yov da bedder wurd, amazkeyatin. Lader I'se tryed ta calls Olive bud shes waddnit yin.

JANDUWARY 25

Disk feelding persisks. Yi'm dincreesinkly nerbus yand yupsed. Olive stild hadsent rekurned me calls, yand so disperyate yam I'se fur reashurinsk dat Yi yakshully conksidyered callink Bluto, sinsk Wimpy yis conkpletesky yunhepfuld. Yin dis statesk Yi willsk nod repurd fur dootsky. No madder yow musk spinask Yi yete yit hads no effecks. Ya cand yan howar dis nodding.

JANDUWARY 30

Mi lowdest pint yed. Wimpy toled mi dat Olive yand Bluto wend yaway toogedder lask weke, yich xplanesk yi shes nod calding mi backs. Yit's nod xactickally a sirprize; I'se suspeckted fur sum tyme dat Olives wuz nunhappee, bud da shocks and hurd yis considskeryable nundelessk. Ifsk yonly Poopdeck Pappy wuzd stilld yalive. Spinask conksumpshin up ta yone cand yevry harf howar. Yi amsk din Hellsk.

FEDUBARY 4

Der yoctor ad de Seemans Hald perperskibed Prozacks. So fur I'se feeld no effeks. Olive and Bluto yar dew basks skoon, perdapsk toonitesks.

FEDUBARY 14

Da Prozacks yas yan inskredyible effecks. I'se feeld bedder den Yi yas din yeerds. Olive yan I'se yad dinnerds lask nite yand I'se toled yer yov howd I'se feeld yand wad da medyicayshun wuz dooyin fur mi. Yand I'se reeliskized howd musk mi beehavyor yin de pask yah ta do wid mi illnesskes. Olive skeemed yappy fur mi. Yi tink she's boodifulsk.

Yand shes toled mi dat Bluto wuz yerry yunattrakive ta hur yin yan yinitmask yenvironskmenk. Nedelesk ta say, Yi wuz gretely cheered, yalmosk uforkicil.

FEDUBARY 27

Yall isk weld. Mi spinask dependeskensk yis yunder konktrol fur da firsk tyme yin mi lyfe. Da Prozacks yis wondafulsk ta me. Tank God fur modernsk mudisen.

AFFERS NODE —

Yi offerds dis yextrack frummed mi privask journalds yin orders dat ovvers wid de samesk prodblems ken takesk hoped frummed mi xperiensk. Rememder dis: Yis dis nod alone.

Yer frend,
Popeye **Q**

The All-Purpose New Yorker *Piece*

When I was a boy in Lapland, my uncle Per placed his warm, heavy hand on my head, as though he were blessing me, and told my mother, "This eaglet will soon take flight." I remember the jolt of surprise which shook me at this remark, for it was the season of transhumance, when the restlessness of the reindeer seemed to sweep through men and dogs, and certainly through boys of fourteen, my age at the time.

I can't say what brought the memory back the other day, here where the drama of the changing seasons hardly exists—I practice neurosurgery in Marin County—except, perhaps, that it was again the time of transhumance, and for a moment, as I watched the fog's daily shrouding of Tamalpais, the traffic below my window seemed to take on the heart-thudding rhythm of hooves on frozen soil.

My uncle Per was a quite remarkable figure in a rather remarkable family—you will soon agree that I do not exaggerate. My mother's side of the family was descended from shamans. But while she seemed to have deliberately expunged all traces of her hieratic past from her consciousness, they still clung to Uncle Per, giving even his minor utterances a haunting authority. This had served him well, I suppose, in his business as an insurance agent in Trondheim. At his matter-of-fact references to the misfortunes to which the human race was prone, illnesses, death, and a wide variety of disasters, the wind whistling around the eaves of his clients' comfortable houses became more menacing and signatures descended swiftly on insurance applications. But he was also very generous, as I was to discover years later when Father refused to support my studies in London and Uncle Per put me on the same footing as his sons.

Ours was, as I've said, a quite remarkable family and much dispersed. Summers, there was always a reunion or two. Almost every summer Uncle Anders would return from Bombay, at first with his Indian wife—I shall always recall her puttering dolefully with her curries over the peat fire—in later years without her. He came back, he said, to escape the monsoons, but our summer mosquitoes and midges made it seem a poor exchange to me. He too was prosperous, in his curio-export business—our winter home was strewn with teak elephants and water buffaloes, to the great bewilderment of our local visitors. "Ah, Bombay!" the pastor would nod affably, but with a gleam of suspicion nonetheless, as though my mother's shamanistic ancestry made him mindful of the need for continued vigilance in our household.

Uncle Anders was not on the best of terms with his wife's family, I gathered. Poor Lapp. "I am homesick," he once admitted to me. It was probably one of the few truths he ever uttered, for he was a notorious fibber. Was he even in the export business? "It has been a very good year in silver," he observed and also mentioned jute. Rather unscrupulously he filled my young mind with terrible fallacies and inaccuracies about India, which I passed on with the innocent confidence of youth at the Nomad School I was then attending. My teachers, poorly trained and insecure, did not quite know how to handle these eye-opening revelations. One said somewhat nervously, "I believe that custom was abandoned some years ago." I had just described in vivid detail suttee, thanks to Uncle Anders. At any rate, when he died, no wife, living or dead, accompanied his body, which was buried according to the custom of our family on the sandy shore of a lake-island. Poor, poor Lapp.

Much more happily do I recall the visits from my cousins Johann and Anna, tumblers in an Argentinean circus. I have seen more skillful tumbling since, I sadly admit, yet they were not without distinction in Argentina. They loved to imitate the ringmaster's introduction, *Y ahora de Lapland*—there are, after all, very few Lapp tumblers anywhere in the world. Their vain hope was to develop a reindeer act—that would have been distinction indeed! They should have known, however, that reindeer are not particularly tractable. One does well to get a harness on them. And even if you taught the stubborn beast to stand on its hind legs, it might bring its front ones down on your skull. Indeed, that nearly happened to dear cousin Anna. But what a time we had as long as they were with us, bringing their gaiety and sense of spangled peril from their magical world! Even my staid father applauded as they did cartwheels on the tundra.

Do not think of us, however, as country bumpkins—dumb-founded, arctic hosts of far-flung relatives smitten with home-sickness. There were return visits too, not to India or Argentina, too far and too expensive, but to Seville in Spain, where another uncle, Nicolaus, had established himself as an accountant for a bullfighting impresario. A far cry, bullfighting, from the reindeer battles he had witnessed as a boy during the mating season! His daughter, who quite charmed me, explained the finer points of the corrida, her hair brushing against my cheek in the *sombra* section of the Plaza de Toros. "There is much mystique about *recibiendo*," she informed me. "Hemingway, you know." I had not even heard of Hemingway, who was beyond the curricular scope of the Folk high school I sporadically attended. It was an unpleasant experi-ence to have one's ignorance exposed in the presence of a beautiful girl. To know so little! But as we strolled in the Alcazar and, later, that evening, in the old quarter near the Cathedral, beneath the hanging geraniums that spilled over the window boxes like melted rainbows, I knew that I loved Elena.

(The fog has settled on the shoulders of Tamalpais, as lush and silvery as a stoat in winter. I blink wearily—four operations this morning, including a rather nasty gunshot wound. Is it the depres-sion of fatigue that makes me probe so grimly amid the debris of my recollections?)

Uncle Nicolaus had a jocund, condescending way with visit-ing kin. He had become quite clever, not only in joshing the folks from home, but also, I was led to understand, in preparing his employer's books for inspection by the tax collectors. "The graz-ing was good this year?" he asked blandly, leveling his hand a ridiculous height above the dinner table. Or had he forgotten amid the orange blossoms how short the lichen grows? "The grazing was fine," I answered rather stiffly. Glancing toward Elena, I sought an elegant way to remind Nicolaus that the herd which carried my own ear-cropping, and which had begun with the reindeer given to me at my first teething, now numbered nineteen thriving head. Nicolaus could be tactful when it suited him. Guessing my predicament, he observed soberly, "It is good that the grazing was good."

We took a short trip to Granada before I returned. Elena, who had seen the Alhambra several times, was bored, but I found it entirely entrancing and marveled at the flair of its Moslem builders, and their wild surges around the Mediterranean, while the Lapps shrank into their arctic barrenness. Elena was wearing the fawnskin vest which my mother had sent with me, exquisitely decorated by her with braid and metallic thread and silver buckles. I stroked the skin, remembering with a pang the fawn from which it had come, and asked Elena whether she would ever visit Lapland. And what, I wondered, could I offer her if she did? Cloudberry, northern lights, and nineteen reindeer. "I rather doubt it," she answered distantly.

When I came home, Father, puffing solemnly on his pipe, inquired after Uncle Nicolaus' health. One would have thought I had just returned from two days at the fair at Jokkmokk, rather than a month in Andalusia. My father pretended, as a matter of principle, that the world beyond Lapland had no reality, except perhaps in my mother's feverish aspirations for my future. As for Elena, she never did visit. In time our correspondence dwindled, somewhat to my relief, I might add. We Lapps are not a very literary people. A saga or two, a minor epic . . .

Also I was much troubled at that time by an enduring disagreement between my mother and father, which was shrugging off its long dormancy like a bear in the spring. It concerned my career.

"And what will he study at the University of Lapland?" my mother asked tartly.

"He will study," my father answered with his pipe-puffing, dogmatic reasonableness, "Norwegian, English, German, calculus, philosophy, economics, zoology, botany, and so forth. How much more does a man have to know to herd reindeer?"

Ah, there was the rub! For nowhere in my mother's vision of my future could any reindeer be seen. But craft and stubbornness were her only weapons in resisting my father's plans and much more of the latter than the former. He would not hear of my going even to Oslo for my education. Perhaps I should say, especially to Oslo, since the capital was, in his view, the breeding ground of all the evil that beset the Lappish universe.

He was in truth a crusty old-timer, and could afford to be as the owner of the largest reindeer herd in Finnmark. A true mountain Lapp, a tent-dweller in the summer, driving two hundred and more head to the richest grazing, let not man nor beast stand in his way. Since all sedentary folk, be they Lapp or Norwegian, were his enemies, he was forever entangled in law. Now he is dead. There are few like him left. And in the long darkness of winter, my dear mother, who alone succeeded in thwarting his will, continues to suffer spasms of remorse.

My own will was much confused at the time—I am by no means certain it has found steadfast peace yet. My father and the life of the arctic hills were inseparable. I loved both. While other pagan people found their early gods in warmth and water and the fertile soil, we Lapps worshiped stones. Perhaps we still do. Why else should Aslak's sons, of my father's family, visitors from New Zealand, have great joy of living with us? They farmed eighty fat acres near Dunedin and found, they claimed, resemblances between the mores of the Maoris and our own, but the lunar harshness of our encampment was kvass to their parched hearts. During the brief summer nights, we lay around the fire like the spokes of a wheel, talking for hours in whispers, and watching sidelong the swift passage of the stars across the *goatte*'s smoke-hole. As the fire burned down, its peaty odor mingled with our own decent human smells and the fragrance of the coffee brewed in vast quantities. Aslak's sons cried when they left.

But let the truth be told—there were disagreeable elements as well in our wild open life. One tires of goat's milk. The midges and mosquitoes I have already mentioned. Nor did I ever become completely adept in the dental castration of reindeer—it was typical of my father to scorn the tongs which the authorities literally thrust into our hands for that purpose.

Ah, the authorities! Culling old papers the other day, I came upon the proceedings of a conference at Karasjok I had attended as a delegate, and I recalled my father's indignation upon reading the provincial governor's speech on my return. "Chiefs of the reindeer administrations . . . the important questions for this second conference dealing with Lapp affairs are education and general culture. . . ." He mimicked the mincing, bureaucratic voices scornfully. "Why don't they let us be, and our reindeer too? They graze where nothing grows except lichen, and we live where no one else will live. We are the oldest race in the world. Even the Nazis did not know what to make of us." Oh, he was angry!

Now that the land of my birth has been overrun by tourists, social scientists, and so-called sportsmen, I thank the Lord my father did not live to see his direst fears come true. My mother, who prospers with her resort cabins and souvenir shops, is more philosophical, yet even in her cheerful letters I see the outcroppings of sadness, like mountain boulders, flesh of the arctic, amid the summer flowers . . .

I traveled. To Costa Rica, to Ankara, to Lisbon. There were always invitations after Father died. "Come stay with us. We have a house on the Istanbul Cadessi. . . . We live well on the Avenida da Liberdad. . . . But for my studies I had chosen England, a free country gentled by its turbulent history. So, in flight and sorrow, I came to the bosom of London, Bayswater. Soon, upon the extraordinary beauty of my feckless wife there fell the shadow of the madness that was soon to quench itself in the foaming mountain torrent at Innsbruck. People would stare at us—at her because, even among the most beautiful women of a dozen nations, she was a creature apart, at me because they had never seen a Lapp before.

My secretary enters.

I rub my eyes to account for their redness. She tells me about tomorrow's appointments and brings the mail. There is a picture postcard of the Field Museum. It is from Elena.

Some weeks ago, crossing the campus of the University of Chicago, where I was attending a neurological conference, I had seen, unbelieving, had followed, hardly daring to hope, the fawn-skin vest, the familiar braid, the silver buckle, wondering bitterly whether these too were now mass-produced in Taiwan (where I had never been). Not until she flung her arms around me and burst into tears could I be sure it was Elena: she was much changed.

We sipped sherry—she Spanish, I Californian—as if to make a point of the distance we had conquered to find each other. Time, however, is not so easily defeated, nor the unhappiness time too often breeds, and there had been much of that in Elena's life. Her father had gone too far, finally, in protecting Don Federico's shady business interests. Costly bribes had to be paid before Uncle Nicolaus, broken in health and spirit, was allowed to retire on a mean pension in Lapland. This my mother had not written—was it to keep me uninformed about Elena too?

After the annulment of her marriage to a Spanish film director she had come to the United States. I asked why. "Why not?" she shrugged. She had worked in the Norwegian consulate, in a Scandinavian bookstore, for an auction house specializing in Eskimo fakes. All of these adventures she made light of, lumping them under the head of "getting by." Nevertheless, "therapy" was mentioned. Her small neat head, gently molded by the midwife at her birth to conform to the Lapp ideal of roundness, turned aside. Her eyes with their faint Mongolian cast became troubled. "And now?" I asked gently. She was taking a master's degree in anthropology. Her thesis was on Stalo, the giant bogeyman of Lapp folklore. "Can you imagine?" She brightened. "My learned teachers take these silly fairy tales *so* seriously."

Stalo, Stalo, do not come to our hearth!
Sleep under the njalla of my enemy,
And I will give you much beer

she sang in the Lapp tongue I was already beginning to forget. The childish melody clutched at my heart. Her own eyes brimmed. "I should be with my old father." But there was apparently a new man in her life, one of her professors, from Pakistan.

"And does he take your silly fairy tales seriously too?" I asked lightly, amazed at the stirring of jealousy. Apparently to change the subject, she asked whether I remembered the gypsies in Granada.

The postcard with the picture of the Field Museum inquired, "Will you perhaps return to Chicago?"

What shall I reply? There are so many places in the world I can return to. Except one, dearest of all, the land of my birth.

In my childhood I had visited a Lapp cemetery. It was many centuries old, going back to the time when it had been the custom to sacrifice a reindeer to the deceased and plant its head upon the grave. What wild beasts could devour was soon gone, so that, approaching the cemetery, one saw only a forest of antlers springing from the earth. It was as though the spirits of our ancestors had assembled, eerily but fittingly reincarnated in the form of the creatures that had sustained their life.

That night I cried out in my sleep, and a moan escapes me now as the memory flares and shimmers, like northern lights, on the horizon of my consciousness.

When will the ghosts of Lapland cease to haunt me? **Q**

Birthday

I don't know what she does in the dark. I bought her a radio and a steak. God must be a good-looking man, she says. She pronounces the French words perfectly from La Boîte du Bois. Pulls on her gloves, fat snowflakes. My sister meets me on the church steps on Tremont Street. We kiss on the lips, cross to the restaurant. It is hard for her to smile in the clay-colored air. Unseasonable damp. We touch hands.

She orders steak medium-rare with onion rings. When she takes off her cap, I see she has cut her hair. Beauty still unspoiled in her face. Pink swatches of evening sunset. I pick at my seafood-stuffed tomato, having purposely ordered something I hate. I wonder at the chemistry in her sterilized body. Satirical womb. Does the birth die out? I want to be all wood and plaster, formaldehyde around the mouth. No different from a frog. Unpeel my body to the gelatinous tiny offspring.

I remember knocking on doors. I remember chasing her down as emissary of the family, to a hidden place where she sat unmoving. The neighbors only said she sat and stared for hours into the dirt rows of garbage. She touched squirrels, threw crumbs to the birds. Once she wrote in a letter, "I took a gray pigeon for a walk today. A sweet-tempered bird, it crouched in my hand while we watched for mallards on the pond." Green feathers in their necks. Blue crowns. Corbeau and sparrow. I remember when our brother died she seized the wall, raised her arms like an animal and swung them down, hard coo broken in her throat. I lay down on three hard mattresses and stared at the holes in the ceiling.

She grew older, left the house. Posed naked for photographers. Click in spine. Older sister, mama, catnip. Leader when we played house. You made me wash the doll clothes till they faded. I grew up hating you. You hid each pink curler. Threw my books into the yard on the hottest days. Made sure the dog had her satin pillowcase at night while we dragged our mattresses down to sleep in the living room. Days you popped green and orange golf balls. Fore, as they went down. On the radio, "Can you really feel it in his kiss?" aired like crazy and you wanted to know. You stole to get everything you could for free, writing letters to customer service reps for peach ice cream and fruit cocktail. Turned the pages of magazines, reading beauty from the lips of models and jars. Pepsodent happiness. Each Saturday, the tight rows of curlers bugled to your head. Your mind a glassy fish bowl, you came pushing through doors, anger in your fists.

Those summers we were stupid, twirling our batons. Lee hung himself from a tree. Now each winter you claim your mind is vacationing in Florida while your body stays home to clean house. The gold sky keeps you afloat. Twenty-seven hard turns into this world today. Blood sisters brought up on nothing. The orphan's eye touched us like a hex. We killed our parents. We die a thousand deaths. We dream. Our tongues are surfboards, words spilling on the tide. **Q**

Circus Station

There it is, and you see the floor, the doorknob, a box you had when you were a boy. Here are his coins in the basket under the mirror. Here is the little wooden doggie on a stick. The table, the plate, and there it is, the hair at first and something small—oh, Lord. Here are the folded bed things, the elephants, the flannel, the stitch. Here are the ruined bed things too, curled and cut. Here is the little wooden doggie in the middle, standing back or land-ing—crashing!—and its rope tail, a brick of the wall, your mother and father sitting in a room. The table, the plate, the spoon, the hair at first, and here is the basket with his coins, with his hat, with his hand, clat and struck. He held glass and chunks of chalk and chips of wet wood. Now you are saying I am old!—a train ride home, horses across the wall in the huff of a field, her stitch, a not-so-thick thicket, his hands along the underside, a day in the rain and here is the way she smelled. The table, the bowl, and here are the blackberries we had for breakfast. You see the door, you see the wall, and they are standing in a room with a basket under a mirror, the burr of a bird, the wood next to the chin. His hand is bent this way. His hand is coming open and there is a twitch of her hair that touches your face. **Q**

Her Best Part

She left as I was cutting the skin from the bottom of my feet with a small pair of scissors. I told her it didn't hurt, wasn't meant to, there was no reason to leave. This skin was hard, dead, almost scaly stuff, built up over the past few months from walking, from shoes and socks and sweat and from our lives together. This is where it all ends up, I told her: here. All the tears, the bad words, our common sadnesses, they drip down our bodies and pool at the bottom, harden like wax, good for cutting. Her feet, though, were amazingly soft all over. Even the big toe, the pad beneath the big toe, while it did not achieve the degree of softness the rest of her foot did, still could only be considered soft, a softness, worth touching, very much worth the touching. And her feet were not her best part, either; she had other, better parts. There were, for instance, her hair and her eyes and her nose and her mouth and the rest of her, on down, ending at not a bad place, a soft place, her feet, sort of orange, sort of pink, it depended on the light, or lack of it. These were the same feet she left on while I was cutting the skin off the bottoms of my own, and, as I said to her, I told her, I did not feel a thing. **Q**

The Difference

Dear Sirs you must know how long I have waited to receive my sent off for object and having yet to receive it am troubled in a way no doubt beyond your job specifications I am writing now for some relief.

Fully aware though I am of the complexities the mechanics the sad numbing routine of the day-to-day you we all are forced willy-nilly to perform it killed my father and though your own situation without question merits at the very least a more sympathetic ear than you may or may not have access to I still must insist in the strongest possible way the delay I have endured to date is entirely unacceptable and I demand your immediate attention to this matter, my wife is very ill. Six to eight weeks the doctors said and that was three weeks ago which it must be a coincidence is how much you gave me too in the beginning and look, how many lives must I grace with my contempt, every drop of blood wrung from my heart like an old rag in her hands I remember, she waits for me now, counting as I am the days.

Dear sirs I placed the order in good faith I fulfilled your terms even the small print I read what more can I do? Picture an old man peering deep into his box with only hope and finding not the sent off for object but other less valuable items and sometimes that darkness nothing at all how long can this really take? Honor my expectation, sirs, my wife is in some pain. And I am aware there are others I am not the only one who has an interest in receiving this object there are millions like me your job is not an easy one my God I told her, we are not special, we are just other people, and yet you would think there would be more to it than this, that it would end up better or different at least, but then we have never really had a clue.

Dear sirs, inside me there is something burning.

And if as I suspect your organization is a large one perhaps my original order was lost this is my wife's suggestion she said it may never have arrived or if it did it was perhaps lost or misplaced or sent to the wrong department or if indeed it was received and packaged and shipped it was sent to an incorrect address my penmanship, she said, leaves something to be desired, something to be desired, she said, my scrawling old clawlike hands. I don't know what to think. She has three weeks now if you can believe the doctors, and I can, looking at her I can, my wife, and in three weeks we'll see, oh yes, we'll see what happens, and I will talk to the doctors about what has happened to my wife at that time. So you see how that explains this letter: I follow up with things.

In closing dear sirs let me just say that whatever has happened and that whatever may happen in the future so help me God I hold no one directly or personally responsible no one person or terrible force in the world for as my wife says her voice as weak as water now the shadow of a whisper I knew what I was getting into when I asked for it I knew, I'm not as innocent as I seem sirs not by a long shot, I have seen many things. And yet I am troubled. My wife is in some pain dear sirs but it's getting better for her lately she has either two or three weeks left sirs two or three weeks left you can't imagine what this imprecision costs us, there is a difference sirs there is a difference, and in a week it will only be worse for us, for her, and in two weeks, well, we shall see then, won't we? We shall see. *Where is my sent off for object?* For I must warn you sirs if it doesn't come soon I will demand a complete refund, a full and complete refund, it is within my rights. This waiting is intolerable but I don't blame you, there is no one to blame only please, dear sirs, if possible I would appreciate your swift attention to this matter. I am writing now for some relief. As always, I am. **Q**

Memory Guy

For starters, I have a confession to make. I have two confessions to make, two things. One of them is that I miss my *old* friends, my *old* life—everything I did and everyone I did it with and everywhere we did it. I remember every meal I have ever eaten and I miss them all equally. I miss five minutes ago. What I'm saying is that I am sentimental and nostalgic. The other thing I forget.

Where I am at right now is on the street, sitting on the curb, to be exact, with my legs sticking straight out in front of me, like the future. My legs are actually in the street, and cars could conceivably come and run over them. I'm waiting for the bus. The bus could conceivably run over my future, too; in fact it's more likely that it would be the bus because the part of the street my legs are in is a bus stop. But the bus is late. People are piling up behind me. It's not the warmest night of the year, but the general attitude here is one of patience and friendliness. No one is ready to kill. Every now and then someone will sort of look at their watch. I have to admit that I moved to the city in the first place because I wanted to see somebody get killed.

The other day a guy was beaten to death by some guys. I was having sex at the time, but later that night I went to the scene of the crime and tried to find brains, a tooth, anything.

I miss eggs.

Today I had three meals: breakfast, lunch, and supper. I remember them. I will never forget them.

I am currently twenty-three years old.

If this bus ever comes—if it comes in the next three minutes, actually—I will make it home in time to pick up a bag of chips at Lotty's convenience store, which closes at eleven.

Everything closes at eleven in this town.

It's ridiculous. My joke is that in this town even the all-night donut shops close at eleven.

My lease expires in two months. I think that after that I will move to a corn field for a few years, not because I don't like it here, because I do. I just also like corn. **Q**

Floodlight

He left town right after high school.

Then he went home and got on at the plant. After a few months he knew he did not want to be an idiot in a bump cap for the rest of his life. The high school principal, an old school mate, got his certification waived, and he started teaching. At first he tried too hard, then he eased up.

The kids were not bad. They made a time line that ran around the room beneath the pictures of dead presidents. He told them about the shift from hunting to agriculture.

The women he had known were mostly gone. Sometimes he went out with a woman from the next town, a fellow teacher. He lived in a bungalow on the edge of town. The house was small and neat, with a yard that gave way to woods. A floodlight was mounted over the back steps, and there were iron clothespoles like equidistant crosses in the yard.

Sometimes he would run into a success story back for a class reunion.

He could not blame the graduates for leaving.

Seemed like a prank when the trouble started.

Someone got him on the mailing list of a firm that sold sex toys. The illustrated catalogue arrived for him at school.

Somebody slashed a tire on his car.

Put a rock through a window of his house.

Took a case of Schmidt that was cooling on the back steps one Saturday night. He had not heard a thing. He got a new bulb for the floodlight. Put out another case and waited in the dark house until he fell asleep in his chair. One afternoon the beer was gone.

His uncle had left a single-barreled shotgun and a coffee can of shells on a shelf in the basement. He went to the sporting-goods store to get a gun-cleaning kit. In the boating department, he found some 12-gauge flares. The man said they could be fired from a shotgun or a special launcher.

He had the window open about four inches. He practiced moving the barrel around in the frame.

He heard something late. Labored breathing. He was not sure it was not his own. He heard something on the concrete steps. He shoved the barrel out the window and fired.

The flare blinded him.

Everything smelled of something burnt.

A man was out there. His foot was caught on the bottom step.

One of the transients from the railroad tracks, the sheriff said. They wander up to the houses sometimes.

His lawyer told him to keep his mouth shut. He did. The grand jury did not return a bill, and he was free of legal entanglements. Completely free to go about his business.

He lost interest in the work. Resigned.

At night he sat at the kitchen door, drinking.

Days, he filled his big green watering jug, wandered among the stones, putting water in the vases and in the cans of flowers. **Q**

This Is It

Sometimes he would watch the news and not know what to think. He said, "I made it, and these other people did not." Perhaps it was all genetic. Other times he rejected the idea that people were wound to attain or to self-destruct. He would shake his head. The television was not that great, for that matter. What did it know? All those shows, for what?

He heard the joke about the president on his television. He told the joke to his wife the next morning. He went to work and told the joke to the fellows there. Scruffy-looking young people came to the house to canvass for the environment. He did not give them any money, but he told them the joke. At the mall, he got the door for a man carrying a box. They had a good laugh over the joke. Later, he told it at the bar.

He went out on the walk and looked hard at the steps and porch. Sometimes people marked houses. Something on the door or a bent stem in the flower bed—anything they could see when they came back later for what they wanted. They knew the code and they had you down, figured, as a member of a certain population. He hoped to find the mark and obliterate it before anyone got to him, before anyone could read it out.

"How much sick time do you have coming?" his wife said.
She thought they should get out of town for a while. It was his fault that she felt this way. She had surprised him in the kitchen one morning while he was pounding it. He realized it was not good for her to see this. "All you do," she said, "is make me sick."

She thought they would do well to rent a cabin in the North. The cabin came with a boat. The cabin had a fully-equipped kitchen and knotty-pine paneling. It sat on a lake in a chain of lakes.

He had worked for years and this was the thanks he got. This and the possibility someone had marked his house and would be around as soon as he was gone.

"Those fish," he said, "they stare at you."

His wife closed the curtains.

By then the boss was on him as well, telling him his performance was slipping, that he needed to take some time. The company had a new policy. They were encouraging people to get out, recharge. The rumor was accrual was on its way out; soon everyone would be forced to take his time or lose it.

He had his own ideas. The carpeting. The fibers emitted toxic materials. And the air-conditioning system was suspect. Who knew what organisms bred in the condensers? He could have thrown that in the boss's face, but he had no hard evidence.

The pressure was too much for him. He buckled.

He found a bump on his scrotum. He felt the bump, rolled it around in his fingers. This was, perhaps, what he had been waiting for. He felt sick and frightened. He had expected the heart or lungs or liver to go first. Some mornings he could feel them going. And now this.

He squeezed the bump.

When he buckled, his boss said, "That's it."

There was no reason for his wife to know. What did she think? That he would sit home with the television, the table, the plates, the household cleaners? She would never understand the office was not his real work.

He went in at 4:00 A.M. and left after everyone else. The door stayed locked and the blinds stayed down. No lights. He told his wife he was on a special project.

He lit a cigarette. "They're giving me the nudge. The kiss

of death is soon to follow." He felt the bump. He wondered who to call. Maybe he could get an implant.

He sat at the kitchen table.

His wife came in wearing her white nightgown. "Why are you here?" she said.

He cocked his head to one side and stared at her.

"Don't start anything," she said.

He just stared.

"What are you trying to pull?" she said. **Q**

Fragonard

Yes, it was just there, what she thought she might call this day, faintly but faintly at the tips of her fingers, the tinily bulbed, split tip of the calligrapher's pen, unsheathed and ready, cradled now in the crook of a finger, along with the white cards. It might be darting too, perhaps, the name she would choose, some fine thing winging among what matter of scattered things, among those names long since faded from her thoughts, darting as the butterfly was darting now, there, in and among the Jennifers and the Royal Appeals. Fitful, it might well be, as those wings and something like those spots, she was thinking, those silky suns daring the jagged edge of a dark wing like somebody's last stepping stones. Her gaze followed the path of the little suns, big to small, to the bottom tip of a wing. She watched the veined petals blink open and apart, letting her see the filigreed furze at their cleft. And was it not being, as it was getting so much to be these days, just this coolly coy, what she might call this day, she thought, the word hovering there like that, indifferent to her, keeping a tight lip on its living bud? Could it today be found perhaps somewhere lingering in the French? *Berger? Bergère?*

Wings?

Wing?

She watched them open and close. She did not move, there on the needled path. She tried to hold them with her gaze, these wings, these fleeting suns, flirting with her eyes.
Names.
Nothing.
This and that.

. . .

She would wait, she thought. But, no. Stop. They were there again, at the Carol Amelia, these little suns, stepping off into nothing, she thought, a brood aback of a dark mother, lost and found, lost and then found again. Jupiter. What did the French say? She wanted to write something down. But nothing was staying this morning, was it? Not the least thing would keep to her lips. Where would they leap to, these suns? Planets. *Vénus*, for Venus, was all that she could remember at the moment. And it was perfectly possible, was it not, that she could probably find some veiled sister of Venus if she looked hard enough through the catalogue. There probably was some new armless wonder, some varietal nursed of a Venus that she could plant. She would not bother to write it down, she thought. She was going to remember. About Venus. About the sister of Venus.

She had had it at the tips of her fingers, some planet, perhaps, in French, but there was no holding these wings, these things gone again aflutter above the babies' heads of the Gretzel. She would keep to the path. They would wait for her, she was thinking—and why could they not? Wait. As she would wait for the right name to come flitting along of its own accord, something entirely appealing and apt, apropos of something to be sure, another George's Delight of a day, something like that or other, nothing mincing or perfunctory, but something truly befitting her, like the right pair of earrings or the right fall of a dress. Not like anything she was wearing now, of course, she thought. Nothing so smack of Cinderella and shoes.

Oh, it was something, all right, just there, nothing that one could see just at the moment, perhaps, nothing that one could put a finger to just yet, but poised. Look at them, poised and perfect, walls of silk, she was thinking. *Chinoise,* didn't they call things like that, or *chinoiserie*? Or something, anyway, not gossamer, she thought. Nothing gossamer about it. But petals, yes, flitting now before her, that someone had perhaps pinched together once and let go their way, weightless and nameless, aflutter of all this that

was hers—such was the name to her, she was thinking, that she
might best bestow upon this day born of a budding sun, this day
of all of her days now growing smaller, silkier, days gone a-maying
and days just slipped and gone somewhere among the Mrs. Cope-
lands and the Sinbad's Glories? Was it not just there, she thought,
just now, the name the morning sun might have first proposed to
her on the porch steps, aflicker in her thoughts, just waiting for the
right mister or miss, the right leafy finger, a perch, a perfect pinch
of what in butterflies they called paradise, as she could be sworn
now to remember, waiting to alight, here, in her garden, awash in
a collector's colors of azalea and rhododendron, the names of the
cultured hybrids inked on little cards in the peculiar slant of what
she thought a mistress' hand might look like at its best, spiked into
the pine chips under each bush?

    The dog was bounding among shrub and flower, careless of
Crest, Concinium and of Mary Yates, pawing for something in
Persia and nuzzling Nile, a curly undulation through the Fortunii
and the Betty Arrington, seen and unseen, a real haver among the
lasses, gunning a run between Flirt and Bangkok, Party Pink and
the rust-edged Sumatra, the Clara Raustein and the Creole Belle.
And was it, this day of hers, to be just something of a moment's
abounding, a dog's day of this early spring heat of a Vulcan's
Flame to bellow up a flush, a Ravel's Rose upon her cheeks and
a sweat in the hollow of her armpits, leaving the jagged edge of
salty stains like a couple of ghosted wings destined for the cleaners
only? Or was it to be flung like the Furnival's Daughter scattered
early, some reckless glove offed no sooner than to be lost forever?
Or was it something one could flatter into staying, with a secret
name whispered, perhaps, into some mistress' artful ear? And
could it not be found, such a name, in all this abundance of her,
clustered here and scattered there in the pure colors of a Mme de
Bruin and the privileged place of an Edith Pride? Was it not, after
all, a friendly sort of day today, the sun, a spot she could feel on
her cheeks, making the piled bags of pine chips in the driveway
into a sort of haycock pitched right out of pastorale, with just the
slightest tinge of imagination necessary—one need only think of

the toile in the bathroom. And did she not have the Windsor Lads aplenty and the Lavender Princesses to make a match, to fetch up a name that she could write tonight in her diary, there, in the kitchen by the window, above the loyal white moons of her Painted Star? Or was this day just another bounder, a haver like all the rest of the nameless days that she failed to remember so clearly, here, now, next to the Adendpodum, another dog day mounting the pines and Japanese maples planted here how many suns ago, burning the slightest salt sweat into her eyes now, nudging up the ball of noon?

No, no. Surely another such name would come, another Count Vitteti Dexter of a day—come to her, as noblesse would oblige it to come, as it were, while she was busy writing the new cards, new cards for the old and torn ones that the dog had had his way with, the Consanguinium rent from the Sanguinium, the Hersey from its Hannah. Surely her day was yet in the best prospect, blank and burning on her cheeks. She stopped down to the Flaming Snow to think another moment and to darken the letters, pushing the dagger of the spiked placard into the soft mound of her belly to buttress the heel of her hand.

But who could think now, in this heat, too early for any given spring that she could think of, and how many times had she told the gardener about water and ink, heat and sun and rain and all the rest? And now, snow. s-n-o-w, she rewrote carefully on the card that had suffered, since water, to grow wings, the pasty-pale, jagged crystal of original blue. How could she, how could anyone think of snow in spring, in heat? And what was he up to now, that dog, anyhow, having his hot hop of it all, Bali to Baden-Baden, the tongue flung out of him without giving up so much as a yap, over there—she could just see the ears, the curls of him now—by the Lem's Aurora, or was it the Toucan, she could not now remember precisely? And yes, she must tell the gardener when he comes to get the snake out of the pile, the snake that gets the only yap out of that dog that deserves a name. Oh, yes! Oh, yes! The snake that she saw just yesterday or the day before sidling under the Jeannie Dosser, or was it the Orbiculare? And this early heat. What about that? she would ask. What would she have to do to stop this bit of droop, to perk these girls up a bit, or was it her eyes only? she would ask. What could she do to pick up skirts around here, and at her age, not yet past stooping, she would remind the gardener, but after all, at her age?

And wasn't the sun having it a bit of his way now with her, high and holy? And wasn't she getting to be a bit of a dish of salt out here already, and the dog, that dog again digging! She must tell the gardener—about the Hess and the Cynthia. And perhaps now was as good a time as any to pounce over for a little pee, before she might have to stoop somewhere by the fence and help that dog ruin her Mardigras. She remembered lemonade. From yesterday or the day before. She would have a little sit-and-think in the cool of the bathroom, a sip at the kitchen table, where she might be able to just put her finger on something before having to come out again into this heat. And the India next time, she thought, and not the wrong jar, so tight to open, beyond anyone's how-not-to-spill-and-spoil-and-stain, she was thinking, as she was tamping the pine needles under the open-toed pumps, worn as a gardener's glove, she thought. Oh, yes, stepping a little unsteadily she was, to be sure, and seeing here and there a little bright path of suns salting the edge of her vision, blooming above the bushes and coned just there among the pines.

She stumbled a little clearing the steps, there by the Trude Webster, grown up to gangling, she thought, by the porch door, and then she stumbled again over the dog, getting a yap out of him as he scurried past her ankles into the cooler air of the kitchen to stop to drink at his bowl. Yes, she could almost see it—after she had placed the cards on the kitchen table, leaving the pen pointing an uncapped, ready finger, and when she had finally stooped to sit, door ajar at the end of the hall—see that wild little tongue, leafed out and lapping at the water.

And she was still thinking, sitting there with the skirt of her sundress edged up at her knees, what she might later call her day, when the sun would have downed, just cresting the Japanese maples at the end of the garden, and of what she would tell the gardener about the Cynthia and the Hess. It was all at the tips of her fingers, she thought, a pinch, a flick of the wrist away. Bowered she was, and thinking just what might be at the lips of the shepherdess, tiny and blue, swinging in the rope swing above her kneeling swain, over and over in the forever world raw-silked on the wall. She was listening to the water that was going and going its way atrickle under her, and listening to the dog, having and having at the pool of water held cratered in his bowl. She was looking at the shepherdess, with skirts all aflutter and ankles kicking up at the upper branches, above the ribbon-tassled bush of the lover's hair. She was thinking about lemonade and about where she would plant the Nursemaid's Elbow, about Jupiter and suns. She was remembering to remember to look up Venus and to order the Always Admired. Yes, she need only wait and listen, listen and wait, and it would come, she thought, the way a mother comes quietly to collect her brood, come and lap her up high and away over the Lydia and Swen, the Auriculatum and the Coral Velvet, the Mme Guillmont and the Boulle de Neige, cradle her up, kicking and singing like some flirting little sister of Venus, high over the Exalted Ruler—Carolinianum, Campanulanum, Degronianum. Come something dark and silky, lilting her into a Languedoc of light, a pure Provence, into the creped, languid arms of the troubadours. **Q**

Altmann's Tongue

After I had killed Altmann, I stood near Altmann's corpse, watching the steam of the mud rise, obscuring what had once been Altmann. Horst was whispering to me, "You must eat his tongue. If you eat his tongue, it will make you wise," Horst was whispering. "If you eat his tongue, it will make you speak the language of birds!" I knocked Horst down and pointed the rifle, and then, as if by accident, squeezed the trigger. One moment I was listening to Horst's voice—"the language of birds"—and the next I had killed him. I stared at the corpse next to Altmann's corpse. It had been right to kill Altmann, I thought. Given the choice to kill or not to kill Altmann, I had chosen the former and had, in fact, made the correct choice. We go through life at every moment making choices. There are people, Altmann among them, who when you have sent a bullet through their skull, you know you have done the right thing. It is people like Altmann who make the rest of it worthwhile, I thought, while people like Horst, when killed, confuse you further. The world is populated by Altmanns and Horsts, the former of which one should riddle with bullets on the first possible occasion, the latter of which one should perhaps kill, perhaps not: Who can say? I felt remarkably calm. I prided myself that moment on my self-composure, taking a minute to sit down next to the two corpses, Altmann and Horst, and to feel the calm to its greatest extent. This calm, I supposed, was not the result of killing Horst but, as one might expect, of killing Altmann. There are two types of people, I thought—type Horst and type Altmann. All people are either Horst or Altmann. I am the sole exception. I repeated the phrase *sole exception*, alternating it with *unique exception*, trying to decide which was the better, and was unable to decide. I flew blackly about, smelling my foul feathers and flesh. I stuttered, spattered a path through the branches of trees, sprung fluttering into blank sky. **Q**

New Killers

Gous and Ramse took turns. Kline stayed in the bathtub, looking out from behind the shower curtain, planning retribution. He wrote what they did on a pad of paper, so as to remember all. When Lux's legs were broken, Ramse took Ping-Pong balls and pushed them down Lux's throat.

Gous and Ramse washed the blood off the bat in the tub. Kline naturally complained—sanitation, after all. They helped him out of the tub and gave him a towel. The three of them smoked cigarettes and talked. Listen to what the assassins said:

One of them said, "What did you think of that?"

One of them said, "A job well done is a job well done."

One of them pointed and said, "Recognize the fine points."

One of them picked something up and said, "This will remain, no?"

Kline knows he should respond. They are waiting for him to respond. They have stopped talking and are looking at him, expecting him to respond. Their attention is focused on Kline, in maddened anticipation.

All the while Kline is worried about how he will remember this. He wants to get out the notepad and write. He keeps his hands where his accomplices can see them. **Q**

Murder, Mystery

Okay, this is a murder mystery. The victim is lying in a field not far from U.S. 36. Face down.

It's early morning. Along the eastern horizon there's a band of clouds, though the sky overhead is blue. The sun is up, but still hidden. Here's what I want you to see: to the west, another cloud bank lies against the Flatirons, with just the jagged tops of the first and third Flatirons jutting through. I've already said the sky is blue, but I don't think you've really seen it. Brilliant blue? Piercing blue? At this distance, you can see the summits of Longs Peak and Mount Meeker, capped with snow and orange in the early light.

See it? See the bright orange mountains against the blue sky? See the clouds hugging the Flatirons? Can you sense what the light is like for someone standing in this field? (There is no one standing there, of course. There's just the body, and the body is lying down.) A western meadowlark sings. They only sing at certain levels of light, early in the day and early in the evening. The song is like this: three bright, slow notes, then a flurry of song too fast and complex to describe. You can hold the sound in your mind for only a moment, then the memory of it melts away.

I know what you're thinking.

We'll get to the body, I promise. But first I want to be certain you can see the light, the two banks of clouds, the orange mountains, the blue sky behind them. It's spring. The foothills are green. Soon the sun will rise a little more and burn those clouds from the Flatirons. You'll see just how green the hills are. The western meadowlark will stop singing.

There's heavy traffic on U.S. 36, but no one has seen the body. Cars swish by. Anyone could spot this body. It's right here in the field.

It looks as if the dead man was shot in the back and fell forward. There's not much blood around the hole in the back of his shirt. The exit wound is probably another story.

Was he killed here? Did he expect it? Were there two men holding his arms while another pointed the gun? What caliber of gun was it? Was he a drug dealer? Witness to another crime? Jealous husband? The lover? Maybe the wife killed him. Maybe he didn't expect it. Maybe he was killed somewhere else and brought here, dumped here.

The soil in the field is soft. There are footprints. Someone will be able to tell the story, or part of it, anyway, by looking at those footprints. They'll figure out the caliber of the gun. They'll identify the man and unravel his history, interview suspects.

But we won't.

This is not that kind of mystery.

His face is against the ground, but turned a little.

At this time of year, at this time of morning, there's something about the smell of earth and growing grass.

The man's lips are parted. His tongue juts a little between his teeth. It's as if he's tasting the dew on the grass.

That's not a symbol or anything. That's just the way it is.

I wish I had a word for the blue of the sky. **Q**

Hippopotamus

"But was it one of the Big Five?" he asked.

He passed her the Dunhill lighter.

She lit her cigar.

He admired the way her cheekbones planed out, lit from below by the gleam of candlelight on the Chippendale table.

"It was a hippopotamus," she said.

She tossed the lighter back to him; it bounced once, then skimmed across the table.

"Where did you shoot it?" he asked.

"In the river," she said.

He sipped his cognac.

She lifted her glass up with her left hand, then swirled the cognac around the rim, around and around.

"Just in the river," he said.

"Just in the river," she said.

"Tell me about it," he said.

He leaned back, put one arm over the empty chair next to him.

"It was taking a bath in the river. We came up in the jeep, and I saw its ears go like shimmy shimmy."

"Shimmy shimmy," he said, and let out a plume of smoke.

"And so I stood up in the jeep and I shot it."

"How did you get it out?" he asked.

"We had to wait three days," she said.

"Why?"

"So the body could bloat up. Then we sent in some *Africanitos* to dive into the river and put a chain around it. Then they put the chain on a truck and they pulled it out."

"Of the river." He smiled. He drank some cognac. He brought his arm back around, then put both his elbows on the table and smoked.

"I'll get the hippo in about five months," she said.

"And what will you do with it?" he asked.

"I'll have frames made," she said.

She sipped her cognac. She puffed her cigar. She admired the way his cheekbones planed out, lit from below by the gleam of the candlelight on the Chippendale table.

"I'll make one little one," she said. "I'll put my picture in it. I'll give it to you for your birthday."

"Thank you," he said.

"You're welcome," she said. **Q**

The Fighter Pilot

An old woman fell into the ocean. Just lost her footing, the undertow catching her by surprise, and the waves began to pull her so she had the sensation of being buried in the sand. She beat at the moving water with thin outstretched arms, and her son came running, kicking and spraying sand from under him. He grabbed his mother's armpits and yanked her upright.

The son's wife came running after him, holding a straw hat on her head against the wind. Husband and wife talked close to the stricken woman's face while they tried to hold her steady. The woman nodded—no, she wasn't hurt—yes, she was okay—as the couple began to walk her away from the water. Her exhausted legs wobbled, what little skin was left on her bones shivered like gray jelly, and she knew she was more afraid than hurt, more afraid of being old and helpless than hurt.

They propped her in a chair facing the waves, her cane dangling from the back of her seat, moving like a pendulum in the wind. She convinced them she wanted to be alone, so the couple went away and left her squinting at the sea.

The tide swelled, sun ablaze, and the old woman sat for the longest time and watched the ocean push its way to her and kept watching the ridge of foam claw its way nearer. It bit at her feet—and when she made the effort to lift herself out of the chair, her muscles turned to stone. It was then that the old woman crouched low, a fighter pilot in a cockpit, and assumed the position of being ready to be swallowed. **Q**

The Glass

They move with the steady, painful sureness of turtles drawn by the moon. "God," he thinks, sitting in his canvas chair, watching. "God, they are huge." They lumber into the ocean without testing it, without looking back, and the foaming water closes neatly around their calves and thighs. They are so big; their legs are like the haunches of animals, but he doesn't mind. He watches them bob into each other, playing and rolling, and it occurs to him that now, in the eye-blue water, they are beautiful. They have become as suddenly and impossibly graceful as two dolphins. "You are very pretty," he says out loud, and the girls touch again, rubbing their swollen arms.

So he is old, but still he has his eyes. He takes a drink from his thermos of very cold water and then sets it back down. He feels the dry sand brush against his knuckles. He watches the big girls jump into the crests of waves, letting the water carry their bodies, coming back up for air in great laughing gulps. He listens to their laughter, and then he closes his eyes and sleeps what he thinks of as his day sleep. When he sleeps on the beach, the sun is black and red and so strong that he imagines his eyelids have almost burned away. He loves to come to the beach.

He sees that the girls are still there when he wakes, just making their way out of the water. The ocean is calmer than before. The girls walk out of it looking tired and clumsy and heavy again. Their big legs are oiled, the skin stretched tightly.

He does not think of himself as a dirty old man, but for a moment he wishes he could be the water that slides from their legs in silky oiled rivers, rushing down thighs and into the soft recesses behind each knee. He shifts his weight in the canvas chair and watches as the girls arrange themselves on their towels. They take small mirrors from a bag and begin to comb out their ocean-roped hair, tugging hard at the knots, and then they put on lipstick, a bright creamy pink, taking it from a pot with their fingers. "You are pretty, but you are fat," he says out loud. Then he closes his eyes and thinks of his wife. He thinks of how she leaned in doorways with a small clear glass in her hand.

Without opening his eyes, he feels for his thermos and raises it up in a toast. "You were a beautiful woman," he says. He holds the cold silver rim to his mouth and swallows.

Sometimes, before he goes to bed, he puts his hand up to his head, rubs his skull, and feels for the leftover heat of the sun. He is very warm and alive. He opens his eyes now to watch the girls. They are lying down on their towels, their backs broad and flat and wide.

The girls are playing at the edge of the water when he wakes up. He watches, pets the soft silver hair of his chest. Their ankles are thick. Their bathing suits shine with the strain of holding their large bodies in. He wishes they would go back into the water. "You have such pretty faces," he says. He pats harder at the fur on his chest. He twists the fur together in short silver curls. He wishes the girls would come talk to him, come stretch their towels near his canvas chair. "Oh, girls," he says, and reaches for the thermos. He hears ice, the way it sounds, clear and forbidding, dropping into a glass. He presses the thermos into his belly. He sees his wife standing in the doorway. He sees the glass.

They are not there when he wakes up from another little sleep. The water in the thermos is warm. **Q**

Catalogue

Dear Buyer,

After so many years, we know you intimately. You abhor the beaten path. Draw yourself a bath and immerse yourself in our pastel-colored bath confetti from France. Wrap yourself in our velvety-soft terry robe of a crosshatched pattern. (Monogramming at a slightly higher cost.) Relax in our grand romantic sleigh bed, handcrafted, handrubbed to achieve a wonderful rosy patina. Make yourself a cup of our specially blended Catalogue Eden tea and sip it from our hand-glazed Italian majolica mugs, set of four, item #G113 in our fall issue. Thumb through these exciting pages. We will not disappoint you.

You'll want a double order of our heart-shaped, hand-tied wreath of shallots from Spain, our succulent Turkish figs, our extra extra virgin olive oil. Our Perugia chocolates make a stunning gift for departing guests.

Spring is traditionally floral in motif, and our stock has been carefully selected to help you continue the tradition in your traditional home.

Remember your grandfather's Panama hat? We've got it. We've got your grandmother's sachets, the ones you used to smell when you peeped in her bureau. We've got the identical linen apron to the one your mother used to wear when she baked her pies. We've even got that Black Phantom bicycle, the one that Santa didn't bring you in 1959. Now's your chance.

Our hand-tinted willow-blossom baskets will bring gaiety to your garden hunt. Vegetable dyes, imported from mainland China. We recommend our café table and chairs supplied exclusively to us by the same manufacturer that supplies the sidewalk bistros of Paris. In pistachio or olive. Your outdoor events will be instantly festive with imported table linens from Arles printed in provincial designs from hundred-year-old woodblock patterns.

Scarlet or royal. Van Gogh himself may have been inspired by these patterns as he sat in a café in broad daylight, remembering the dimensions of the starlight, with the colors of the cosmos wheeling in his mind.

From Provence we bring flowerpots that retain the character, form, and rich green color of antiques. Though they are the kind of thing that you see abandoned at the edges of cemeteries in France, in your home they can acquire a new distinction. Anyone who has ever been to France will recognize them as the ones the flower vendors on the Left Bank use. They are hand-thrown at a 19th-century pottery, and we will sell them to you at a price that would be enough to house a homeless family for a month, or feed for a week the family of Turkish refugees who made them especially with your lifestyle in mind, not the one they will ever have.

We have a stunning amaryllis in a Foshan pot, and fragrant paperwhites in a bamboo box. Our *pièce de résistance* is a dramatic wreath of handmade strawberries, currants, raspberries, and grapes that are unusual in their realism and lightly scented. You may want to display it prominently in a kitchen or centered on a small table in your breakfast nook to be appreciated by your departing guests.

To add depth and dimension to your garden, we recommend a special package, "The Garden at Giverny," six seed packets of easy annuals imported from France: morning-glories, wallflowers, hollyhocks, nasturtiums, poppies, and sunflowers, with special marker stakes to denote to departing guests that these are not the same as the ones that bloom perpetually along the beaten American path. To provide form and substance to your normally one-dimensional garden we have *tuteurs*, sturdy steel structures that the French import from Indiana to force flowering vines into more desirable shapes. To force your stature in Chapel Hill or Charlottesville into a more desirable shape, we recommend the entire Monet collection. Gift package available.

Create your own sea of tranquillity with our Japanese mountain garden collection. Make your own path with rain-beaten flagstones, no two alike, found at the base of Mt. Fuji. We will even explain to you why you must not say "Mt. Fuji*yama.*" We know you fear redundance. For an alternative to the conventional, try our rain drain, borrowed from the traditional Japanese, and provide a watercourse for rain to cascade gently to the ground.

Our Chinese porcelain jardinieres are unusually colorful, elegant, and free-spirited, quite unlike the drab-coated, faceless people who make them. You can display them on your terrace with our Japanese-made courting doves, sold on page 34. You can possess these reproductions of museum pieces that depict more graceful times. You can own these fully-glazed, cobalt-blue vessels with Chinese folklore symbols that will be meaningless to you until you read the brochure that our writers have thoughtfully prepared with you in mind.

We have majolica cachepots from Italy that approximate the copies the English artisans made to resemble the poppies of Iceland. Colors: periwinkle, peach, starlight, jade, prairie, smoke, cosmos, beet. These bear a striking resemblance to the very ones you innocently threw out of your mother's house when it was time to close it, when she began wandering the path along the interstate in the starlight, beaten, apron awry, the cobalt meaningless in the blue vessels of her paper-white skin, following the sound of the memory of your first cry.

It was a distracted time for you, we understand, to move her to the Mountain Garden Rest Home in Paris, Tennessee. How could you have known that already our buyers were scouring the dimestores of Italy to bring cachepots especially to you a year later at considerable cost?

You can water your periwinkle and cosmos with cans that come from Portugal, England, or Denmark. They are so beautifully hand-enameled that you may want to display them prominently to enable you to distinguish yourself from your neighbors. We have Delft flower bricks crafted especially for us by Dutch artisans who stole the designs from Venetian vases that were copies of ancient Chinese designs from dynasties that drowsed for thousands of years, no two alike. Authentic reproductions.

We have things for which the names exist only in languages you do not speak. We will not desert you. We know your hungers. *Jacquard, jardinieres, étagères, trompe l'oeil.*

Your lover is only available in limited quantities to bring gaiety to your garden hunt. We offer our Amish wedding quilt, fifteen stitches to the inch. Picture yourself picturing yourself specially blended in authentic reproduction with *something* that has remained genuine or durable or good, like a sun-ripened Amish girl or an earth-scented Amish boy, extra extra virgin. Imagine this instead of only yourself exquisitely handrubbed to achieve a rosy patina to your complete satisfaction.

We know that your children will enjoy our handcarved hand-painted handpicked handthrown dollhouse accessories.

Larch and pine, birch and mahogany. Tropical teak, resistant to rot and termites. Some assembly required.

You may want to display our hand-pickled vanity mirror prominently in your foyer with our paper-white narcissus, sold on page 20. Picture yourself suitable for framing.

Sometimes your footsteps flag upon the stones of your path. The festive colors of the cosmos are suspended in your mind. You are colorless and odorless and beaten and stunned. No two alike.

We dispatch fleets of flights.

No assembly required. **Q**

No, I Am Not a Lumberjack

Do not tell anyone, but the Head Sister told me that they hire the kickers here because they are hard kickers. The Head Sister also told me that the kickers are not hard to find. Still, I think it is safe for me to say that the kickers are hard kickers. They will not kick me without the wood box. This is fine with me, having no quarrels with the kickers. They kick when they kick, and I am happy to crouch on my stool to be able to stare through the open slit of my window at the kickers kicking the wood box. The rest of the window sadly being opaque from way back. It would not surprise me if the others were crouching fast by their open slits too, to watch either the wood box or the kicks or the kickers, or any combination of the three. I am not a wood man. But I tell the others, better to crouch fast on the stool to watch the kickers kicking the wood box than to endure what the sisters call playtime, or hobbyhorse, or chalkboard. Everyone who knows knows that what sets our hearts to fluttering sits in the swift motion of the kick, or in the contact that the kick makes with the wood box, or in any other of the thrills that can be got with the wood box, or from the kicks, or from any other cadence that can be acquired from the kicking therein. Better, I tell the others, to have a stool sliver split the skin of your fundament than to let them drag you away from your stool to join the sisters playing fish, or fishing about for things to confess to kick about. But better being beside the point because the kickers are not bad kickers. I think I would not get into trouble with them were I to say so. One could even go so far as to say that they kick from heel to toe, from heel to toe, from heel to toe, without rest, starting at the top front of the wood box. It would not surprise me were I told the front top of the wood box was claimed by another to be the back bottom of the wood box, or some other such thing. No, this would not surprise me. Nonetheless, the kicking still starts at that kick point of origin where the so-far uncrackable skulls lie. Thank god or me for the wood box, or any combination of the one. Kicking, then, to what has been dubbed the scrotum knot, that place where the scrotum itself lies scrunched tightly in the safe haven between thigh and thigh. For, you see, they put live creatures in the wood box. Then, kicking on, with no opportunity yet untaken to kick again. Over the knees, the ankles, then around to the bottom back of the wood box, or the top front, perhaps, where lie the soles of the quivering feet. Yes, one could say that. One could say that and not be held responsible for what one said, which, when all is said and done, is not half bad. This being not the half of it. But onward to the matter of the wood box, certainly not forgetting the kicking or any part of the process therein, all the while fending off the urge to speak about other kickings and goings, first principle in this place being that it is not wise to let yourself be robbed of the wood box, or of the opportunity to talk wood box, the wood box being a hard place and no less easily come by. With plenty of kicks still to come, but for brevity's sake, let me just say that it is a simple wood box, gathering, perhaps, undue attention. A wood box freed from the funereal frills of thick coats of black lacquer or of black-veiled mothers or of grieving sons. A wood box freed from all unnecessary shapeliness or from doodads or from the craving to be a wood box a wood box is not. A merely able wood box, one might say. A functioning wood box. And a not unhandsome wood box at that.

Wood is not my specialty, but I do not think it is wise to pay out good money for wood to have it kicked and left with deep dents or big chips or long cracks or a slight deformity of the upper regions, that place where the so-far uncrackable skulls lie. Not to mention the hiring out of the kickers or of the wood box builders, who, the Head Sister insists, do not come cheaply these days.

Yet, the desire persists to talk on about the wood box from the vantage point of my stool and slit. Let me add that the talking on this way allows me to talk on further and at length and width, leaving out, of course, the depth, for no nimble kick has ever come from this. Still, it must be brought forth that every thrill does not sit solely with the kickers, nor in the contact that the kick makes with the wood box itself, these being only part, not parcel, of the package. A shift of eye, or even a full bone crank of neck, reveals a pre-box pre-kicking of no less preponderant effect. One might even go so far as to surmise that to crouch here on the stool provides no firm fundament from which to shift the course of their kicks, be it a kick at skull level, or at scrotum knot, or at the soles of the quivering feet, or at some place in between, the choice being theirs and no one else's but.

And has issue even been taken with the kickers' recourse to kicking? None such luck, I imagine, being no lumberjack come down from the North to chop a path clear, no matter what the Head Sister may have said, and in no wise quite ripe for the task. The point being, again, and alas, that I think it is safe to say that the kickers are not bad kickers, and to ask you what earthly use would I have for a stool were they not? **Q**

Home, School, Office

I remember buying something once—I can't remember what—in the stationery aisle of an all-night drug store, something I didn't need. All I remember is what the card on it said: "101 uses for home, school, office." I remember thinking that there was a home, a school, an office in my life, so why not?—make the purchase, look alive. This was how long ago?

HOME

The home in this case was actually two homes. First, my apartment, which was a kind of enclosed hobo jungle—just mounds of dirty clothes, newspapers, index cards, depilatories, and paper plates forming a ragged little semicircle around wherever I happened to be sitting on the floor when I was home. (I had no furniture; alone, I was afraid of heights.) And then her place, a house she rented, a place she vacuumed and dusted, where I slept with her, where she made the bed. She had a name, a job, kids, ex-husbands, relatives. When she wasn't drunk, I was her project.

SCHOOL

I taught at a school, a college—actually a community college. The students hated me, and most who got stuck in my courses eventually dropped them. When I stepped into a classroom on the first day of the term, at least a third of the students, furious upon realizing that I was going to be the teacher, would get up and walk out. On those who remained, I got my revenge by dishing out all A's—even an A for the kid who slept through my entire last term, because I was jealous of his frictionless, rubber-limbed sleep. I'd often want to stop talking—there was never any discussion; I filled the room with words for 50-minute periods, displacing the air with sequences of crumpled syllables arranged to give one the feeling, afterward, of having heard something like a lecture, something that could survive on a margin-doodled notebook page as a plausible outline of a plausible topic—so that I wouldn't wake the kid up, even though he could obviously sleep through a disturbance of any kind. (My own sleep was and continues to be a risky business—scraping, choppy, unproductive.) Shall I admit that more than once I wanted to share that kid's sleep— i.e., to be fucked and fucked and fucked by him until I bled?

OFFICE

I shared what had once been a large supply closet with a history teacher, a woman who smelled like the exhaust fumes of a bus and who often canceled her classes. One morning, as I was repositioning books and papers on my desk, an elaborately coiled pubic hair—it reminded me of an ampersand or a treble clef—slid out of a folder labeled "To Be Filed" that I had been finding a new place for, and landed on the pavement-colored carpet. My officemate wasn't around, and the office door was shut, so I got down on my knees and looked for the hair. I thought it would be easy to find, but it wasn't. I couldn't find the thing. I got a piece of tape from my officemate's desk (I had never asked for any supplies, but my officemate had a metal tape dispenser, a stapler, and lots of other office supplies that anchored her in the office, even though she rarely showed up) and thought that if I dragged the tape, with the adhesive side down, along every square inch of the carpet, the hair would eventually stick to the tape. But after about five minutes, I gave up—not because the phone rang (the phone never rang) or because there was a knock on the door (I had five office hours a week, but nobody ever came by except students seeking my officemate), but because I did not know up to what point, to what extent, I was going along with my life. **Q**

Speak Up

She wants to know what he saw in her, so I reach right in for it, pluck it out, and hand it to her. It's a grammatical occurrence of something big, something way out-of-scale.

This is a conversation we're having, an incident. She is hemming his trousers, the six pair he left behind. I have been encouraging her to wear them—one pair per day of the week, time off on Wednesday, middle of the week, in case she runs out of anecdotal material.

In short, I tell her, hate him.

But she wants to know what if he calls, what if he comes back, what if they're both shopping in the same supermarket.

Skip it, I tell her.

To be fair, what goes where? In terms of my life, where should this be taking place?

The only way this keeps going is if you speak up.

Tell me something.

Tell me every little thing.

How's every little thing? **Q**

This Story

This story has two parts.

The first part is about his last love—how he got circumstanced in it, and all the deodorants and coupon specials and curfews and abbreviations that it involved. The first part is long—much too long for me to include or even summarize here—and it raises issues of gender, class, and race. Please do not hold it against me if I pretend that this part of the story was misplaced or forgotten. I am already ashamed of a hundred other things. (For example, I am a compulsive biographer. I am writing an unauthorized autobiography. My bowel movements are merely rhetorical.)

The second part of the story is short and familiar. It parallels your own life, so it's easy to remember. It lends itself handily to group discussion. I will recite it in its entirety:

Mom, you cunt! **Q**

Employment

I'm looking for work in this room, naturally. I'm desiring lots of work in this room. I'm very serious about my desire.

I go up to the guy. "Is there work?" I ask.

"I would imagine," he says. "Can you start today?"

"Right now," I say.

He shows me to the desk. It's the same old desk, my desk.

I pull out the chair and sit down.

I open one of the desk drawers and find my underwear and socks exactly where I always keep them. I open another and find my health and beauty aids.

Before I can open another drawer, the guy says, "You get dental, eyeglass, life insurance, major medical, death and dismemberment, disembowelment, two weeks paid vacation, seven paid holidays, fifteen paid sick days. Employee pilfering is the retail sector's dirtiest secret. Lift with your whole body. Be a people person. Follow these instructions for filling out your time sheets. From now on, use the employees' entrance. Report all accidents, no matter how small, to the management person. This concludes the orientation program. You may self-start now."

I reach for a pen. He slaps my hand.

"Just do whatever you usually do," he says. "Only now it's going to be work." **Q**

The Grant

I received a grant to develop a treatment program for poets who write about "the dark."

My intake person admitted the first half-dozen.

I handcuffed them in a circle around a mercury-vapor lamp.

When the words kept slopping out, I had to hire three-year-olds to shine flashlights in their eyes. **Q**

Tyke

She was blonde, beautiful. She played the piano. She wrote poetry. She had been an actress, had excavated a Mayan ruin.

Her husband edited a newsletter. He wrote books about the poor, about drug addicts. He had lived with Indians. He and Marcia lived in a small house. They had a son. On weekends they worked at a hospital for children with AIDS. Marcia held the babies and wept. At night, they held hands and talked. The human race would be better. Their child would be a good person. It would make a difference.

The cab pulled up.

Tyke got out. He was bald. He had small eyes. He was a cook on a freighter. He had stabbed a man to death in a fight. His mother had hanged herself. His father had disappeared. He had decided to eat Marcia.

"That is not nice," she said.

Marcia smiled.

Tyke opened his mouth.

There was a sucking sound.

Marcia left her feet.

Tyke swallowed, spit out a shoe, got back in the cab. **Q**

Automobile, Watchdog

Automobile, thin leaflike structure of elastic cartilage that rises at the root of the road and forms the front portion of the entrance to the ocean, home, or empty space. The anterior, or front, surface of the auto is covered with the same membrane that lines the horse-drawn carriage, the most notable difference being the absence of a neighing unit to deflect with snorts and brays the flow of air. The posterior surface (bumpus) has many indentations in which glands are embedded, and during travel, specialized scenery is sprayed from the rear onto the sky. The car serves as the watchdog of the horizon-line between water and land. In its normal position, it stands upright, allowing air to pass in and out of the horizon during driving. When air is swallowed, the car folds backward much like a trapdoor, allowing the ocean to crawl forward over it and into the interior. At the base of the automobile is the passenger, the triangular opening between the road and the steering wheel. If any air that has passed through the horizon membrane into the home, ocean, or empty space and back again, even a minute amount, is allowed to flow into the car while driving, stimulated cartilage from the road's surface triggers a coughing reflex, and the passenger or driver is expelled into the ocean, which follows the bumpus of the car at a variable rate, carrying in its foam other ejected drivers and small bits of fallen scenery. **Q**

Accountant, Vessel of Notice

Accountant, vessel in which a substance is heated to a high temperature and then transferred, divided, shrunk, or counted. The process is a simple heat census which serves to enumerate and refuel specific people and currencies, briefly recognizing or shrinking them before forgetting them entirely. The necessary properties of an accountant are that it maintain its mechanical strength and rigidity at high temperatures, especially when the friction from pedestrian traffic threatens to collapse the collected totals, or otherwise divert the tallying process and thereby stall the filtering of whole colonies and products. ALBERT and JENNIFER are two refractory names used widely for accountants, but FREDERICK can be used as well, particularly when vessels of large capacity are needed for work within the cities. Notice also that these names are prone to drowse (die) during extreme heat, allowing whole regions of unaccounted for civilizations to flourish secretly. Counting single objects, or totaling a group of previously counted items, generally causes lapses in target-oriented behavior, also called the "Boneless Ethic"; for this reason the vessel is handicapped with a lack of desire, which usually curtails any suspicion of stupidity in the accountant, although mustaches and wigs often counter this safety valve, and lend greatly to puppetlike movements made for no reason. Furthermore, the mustache and wig are charms for wakefulness when used as insulating devices. Still, there are moments when the heat inside the vessel of notice escalates beyond the safety of these parameters (sneaks through the hair), and Albert, Jennifer, or Frederick, usually in circus costume and sidetracked, becomes paralyzed on the road, while a stream of burnt figurines clutching money and singed hair walks forth onto our streets, uncounted and never before seen, skidding past their sleeping god, where they mix with the water and air, building colonies of money inside a new, miniature weather. **Q**

Intercourse with Resuscitated Wife

Intercourse with resuscitated wife for particular number of days, superstitious act designed to insure safe operation of household machinery. Electricity mourns the absence of the energy form (wife) within the household's walls by stalling its flow to the outlets. As such, an improvised friction needs to take the place of electricity, to goad the natural currents back to their proper levels. This is achieved with the dead wife. She must be found, revived, and then penetrated until heat fills the room, until the toaster is shooting bread onto the floor, until she is smiling beneath you with black teeth and grabbing your bottom. Then the vacuum rides by and no one is pushing it, it is on full steam. Days flip past in chunks of fake light, and the intercourse is placed in the back of the mind. But it is always there, that moving into a static-ridden corpse that once spoke familiar messages in the morning when the sun was new. **Q**

Landing on Floating Island of the Gods

Landing on floating island of the gods without invitation, form of deafness exemplified by reckless flying. The flyer is within the wind, is an aspect of human weather. When one of the senses is stalled, a form of deviant weather occurs where the wind's bits (flyers) do not adhere to the arc of their origin. This causes all kinds of crazy landings. The particular deafness spoken of here effects breaches formerly unheard of; the flyer will glide unknowingly past the warnings of others, he will focus only on a lush strip of green and gold earth seemingly floating in the middle skin of the atmosphere. The gods are there. With closed eyes they are frying tiny birds over a fire. Then from the sky a man hurtles downward, the sound of the gods washing past him like colored wind, his fingers twisting in elaborate shapes of speech. The gods turn their heads into the smell of the roasting food, their dream erased by a dark rupture in the sky. **Q**

Snoring, Accidental Speech

Snoring, language disturbance caused by accidental sleeping, making a person speak in compressed syllables and bulleted syntax, often stacking several words over each other in a distemporal deliverance of a sentence. The snoring person can be stuffed with cool air to slow the delivery of his language, but perspiration froths at key points on the hips and back when artificial air is introduced and thus the sleep becomes sketchy and riddled with noise. It is often best to cull the sleeper forth from static communication by responding to his snores with apneic barks, sounds made without using any air. The effect of the barks is to isolate each aspect of the snore-sound by slowing down the delivery. In a sense, riding the sleeper until the snore breaks into separate words. Decoders should sit on the bed and jostle the sleeper's stomach. This dispatches the clusters that often form when the sleeper speaks all at once (snores). The decoder is then better able to decipher the word blocks. When analyzed, the messages are simple. Pull me out, they say, the water has risen to the base of my neck. **Q**

Hidden Ball Inside a Song

Mutilated Stephen on horseback chased into forest, a game referred to as the hidden-ball game or the bullet game by some analysts. We know that certain people will chase circular objects when a song is played; the wider the song's structure, the longer the person will hunt for the ball, stone, or bullet. Built into each song's melody is a capacity for mutilation which can only emerge when the lyrics are excluded (the melody's force is often muted by nonsensical words rattling at the surface). In hidden-ball, when the lyrics are forgotten (due to irretrievable dance steps that erase our memory for words), the melody slips unbridled to the foreground and crushes the horseman's torso. This often happens at the periphery of a town, where musical residue gathers more easily since people are very often silent when entering or leaving a town. Chatting naturally decreases the music's power; therefore the activity is performed with silence. Efforts to cheer are suppressed into dances or other occupations that distract people from speaking. Hidden musicians dot the landscape and emerge from the sand with boxy stringed instruments as soon as the riding Stephen is encircled. As previously seen in the *Arkansas 9* series, games of musical mutilation last as long as musicians can sustain the song's repetition, inventing songs within songs when the need arises. The Stephen, particularly prone to crushing, is aimless on horseback by definition. The technique is to get him thinking ball when there is no ball, to surround him as he's mutilated by the song and just beginning to search for a bullet, a pebble, a walnut. The forest should have been previously scoured of all things round, yet it should remain as the only possible field of search for the Stephen. This is achieved easily. He'll be stupid, crushed, bleeding. Circular decoys (not actually round; inflatable, made of straw) should be littered in abundance at the edge of the woods so he'll race there with a greedy mouth. Still, the musicians must always be careful not to end the song too quickly, celebrating before the impossible cycle of the search is fully initiated. There is the further danger of drawing other horsemen into the fold by over-amplifying the music and externalizing the lure. Teamed Stephens can easily find roundness where others cannot, so guards can prevent the intrusion of extra horsemen by dampening the field of sound with water skins, enclosing and further strengthening the one Stephen's playing area. As the song escalates, skinning down around the forest like a horizon squeezing up the land from all sides, the only roundness is the mutilated Stephen's eyes circling freely inside his boneless head like a voice behind a wall. He is horseless on his knees beneath a whirl of pitches and tones in the center of the forest, looking for something he already has, and the song opens up further and closes and opens and shuts down closed and open in a circle of noise around him. **Q**

Swimming, Strictly an Inscription

Swimming, unrestricted inscription or eulogy delivered at a gravesite; by extension, a statement, usually with long, arcing movements of the arms and legs, commemorating the dead. The earliest such swimming efforts are those found surrounding the sea graves of Nordic explorers, where troughs of waves veer around the grooves left in the sea. Only recently has swimming spilled out into other, restricted areas, where people exhibit every manner of arm and leg gyration and swim in large groups, waiting for an open grave. **Q**

Coughing, in Human Beings, Device

Coughing, in human beings, device for transporting people or goods from one level to another. The term applies to enclosed structures of the throat as well as open platforms used to provide vertical transportation within cars and while lying in bed; it is also applied to devices consisting of a continuous belt with attached buckets for handling bulk material. Simple throat-hoists were used from ancient times, often retrieving people whose whereabouts had been unknown. This retrieval can be halted if any of the human air ports are obstructed, causing limbs of the body to inflate or swell during coughing. This is called expanded house and, in effect, increases the area a person has available to himself to hide in. For effective retrieval, the coughing must be focused on a specific limb and requires an exact, crouching posture of the cougher. Otherwise, the hiding person will vanish inside the boggy limb from one place to another, skillfully avoiding the suction of the cough and remaining undetected. **Q**

How I Saved the Day

Someday I will have to let her down easy. On a day like today—when any break in the silence is welcome. She has learned to follow the old advice and say nothing. So I said, "We'll go to the beach. We'll go early tomorrow and have lunch coming home."

When we woke, we were touching.

The people we had wanted to be on the beach watched us arrive. We walked in the soft sand in our shoes. I stopped where the blankets had thinned. I tried to pick out her approach in the swarm. She came up behind me.

"If I had sat down, you wouldn't have seen me," I said.

"I saw you," she said. "I watched you the whole time."

She had gone down to the hard sand. She could not have watched me without stepping on bodies.

"Is this what you want?" I said. "You want me to leave you behind?"

"Do what you want," she said.

"If I'm leading, I want you to follow," I said.

"Don't take me into account," she said. "Go as if you were alone."

So I went. I saw the bodies. I made sure she could see I was seeing them all, ripe and overripe, flesh falling off the bone. I watched the children too, not so much for what they were but for what they would become.

Even if today is not the day, I will remember the bodies lying under the sun, how the people I wanted to be left early, how they took up their chairs and gave up their spaces, how the breakers threw body-surfers back at the shore, and children ran screaming from the tiniest waves. The mothers ate fruit they had brought for the children. Juices ran down their chests. A child dropped his ice cream in the sand, washed it off in the surf, threw it away.

I knew she had lost me. She had left her sunglasses and shoes. Her wallet was there in the bag. I watched for a woman walking the beach, not wanting to appear she was lost. Of all the women, I saw her the most, defiantly pale, hair pulled back and breasts spilling over her suit, a pigeon-toed walk and the fingerprinted corners of her eyes. She would be staring at where she remembered the blanket. But the spaces were filled now. Everything had changed while she was gone. I wanted to keep the place just as it was. I thought I should leave a space on both sides of the blanket.

But say, by a landmark, the lifeguard's chair, she had marked where the blanket was. If I moved, she might assume I had gone. And why wouldn't I—because we had come so far? The only reason to stay was to know that at least I had stayed.

I had expected her whiteness to appear like the moon. But when I watched for her, all the skin that I saw was white, and then all I saw was her face, pointed above the blanket, her eyes with the furrows not seeing me—that's what I saw. But I could not match what I saw with what I saw on the beach.

Her book, her blanket, her lotion, her shoes. The clothes she took off, unfolded. Her money, her wallet. I went down to the water. It was not far. When I found the blanket, the blanket was empty, except for the shoes and clothes, her book and my book.

I had been reading when she went down to the water. She washed her arms and her face. The waves curled brown near the shore. There was no coming out of the water without dredging herself in the brown.

I could feel the earth being gnawed by the breakers. Some people went out to meet them, and the breakers would carry them in, in the foam. They stood up then, where the foam turned to brown in the wash of the weeds, as if they were born again. They had given themselves up to the waves, and the waves gave them back after taking them into the foam. It was just luck, I think, that those people came back.

But whatever the breakers take must be returned.

Or there would be no beach.

Marriage is like that—take, in rage, and give back, day after day, in infinitesimal depositions that make up for days like today. How would it be to leave and be left?

I did not leave. But I saw women with whom she could not compete, and she must have seen men less common than I.

There must be a thing that I'm missing. It was there on those days when I looked at women and found that they had been looking at me. Before I knew her, when I looked, they had always turned away. But on those days, I turned, back to her. She made me more than I was. When others saw just what I was and were ready to discover I was less than my appearance implied, she knew I was more.

And I was.

She was just a head, out there, in the water. The bodies were on the beach. I had seen them, yet I had turned away, but I had not turned to her. I had turned to the book. What I did not want to see most was her face.

She will see when she comes. Because when other people turned away, I looked for her, and everywhere I looked was the sun. So now I have this face. It feels, beneath my fingers, like someone else's face, someone who forgot he had a face and left it out in the sun.

She should have seen me. Maybe she did. I was the person stomping the length of the beach. I was the person who looked at every other person to make sure that person was not her. Every person on the beach knew her name. Women who fit her description were asked if her name was their name.

The rest of my body was saved, but these feet and this face were burned. Women and children watched me burn on the blanket, as lifeguards called her name, and looked at heads in the water, and waved people in near the shore. Once, they charged through the waves and threw out floats tied together with rope. I went to the hot dog stand, to the man selling Popsicles. I stood in the lot with popcorn and wrappers and glass all around and people walking gingerly by, and each time I looked at the people, they were looking at me. Before they could look away, I looked away. I looked from one to the other, then I looked in the cars. My car was still there. Every time I looked at the blanket or car, even if I had just before looked, I expected to see her. I knew how she would appear, tired and pale, and waiting for me to say I could never love anyone but her, that all the bodies and women are the same, to me, as the bodies and men are to her.

I searched through the faces for a face that was searching for mine. In all the places I looked, I looked back to where I had been. She could have been so close that I had looked beyond where she was to where I thought she should be. I looked in the car. I saw a face in the car window, my face, searching for her in my face, and seeing nothing I wanted to see. All the times I had looked in the mirror, I had seen what I wanted to see. When what I saw was not what I wanted to see, I saw how my face was changed. This was the face she had seen.

Then she had gone to the water.

Then I went back to the blanket. She was not on the blanket, and not on the beach, and the lifeguards were watching the water, which had begun to recede, taking whatever it took from the beach out to sea. The blankets around our blanket were gone. It was as if we had just laid down the blanket, stretching it out in the sand. Her shorts were still in the shape of her hips. She was not in the parking lot. She was not in the bathrooms. She was not on the road. The lifeguard said someone had seen someone like her on the beach.

"Was she pale?" I said. "With freckles on her nose and shoulders? Did they notice her breasts?"

"Her hair was tied back, her suit was gray, that's all we know," said the lifeguard.

"Is there someone else here who saw her?" I said.

"The person who saw her is gone," said the lifeguard. "I took the report and passed it to the other lifeguards. We're keeping an eye on the crowd, but there's no one who fits that description."

"Where did she go?" I said.

"The person who saw her is gone," said the lifeguard.

"But where did the person go who might have been her?" I said. "A person with nothing cannot disappear."

"I don't know, sir," said the lifeguard. "That's it for now. That's all we can do."

"She was pale," I said. "She'll be sunburnt by now."

I rolled up her bag and her clothes and her shoes in the blanket and threw them away. I took the money from her wallet and went to the lifeguard, who was high in her chair, with her glasses off now.

"I can't accept that, sir," said the lifeguard.

"I know," I said. "I'll leave it here in the sand. When you come down, pretend that you found it."

"Here it comes," she said.

A helicopter. **Q**

Rules

The first rule was that whenever he came to a red hand at an intersection, he had to stop, look around, and travel in the direction of the first walking man he saw. The second was that if he reached the center of the street—the yellow lines—by the time the walking man disappeared, he could finish crossing; otherwise he had to go back to the corner and begin the process again.

Though this may seem an elementary method to proceed by, it had its complications. For example, when he found an intended direction of passage blocked by a red hand, the logical plan was to look only in directions that led where he wanted to go, and avoid looking in all others. Simple enough. However, he was frequently tempted by the allele we collectively inherited from Lot's wife, which ensures that the more we tell ourselves not to do something, the more likely to do it we become. Thus, even the quickest unintended glances could take him five or six blocks out of his way before he finally regained control of his bearing.

As if these two rules didn't require ample concentration, they were increasingly complicated by cumulating new rules. The worst had created itself: it said any time he even *thought* of a new rule, it became a new rule. You can imagine the impact this rule had on the game, considering the aforementioned allele. To counteract it, he learned to preoccupy his mind—engaging in difficult division problems, or reciting the alphabet backward. But the latter of these techniques didn't last long, as its repetition allowed him to do it in less and less time and with a decreasing degree of focus, so errant thoughts could find occasion to slip in between letters (q and p, for instance), rendering the effort ineffective.

One such slip bore the bus rule, which said if he came to a bus stop where a bus waited with open doors, he had to get on and ride exactly three stops before getting off.

Needless to say, he was often late for work. **Q**

Homework

New ones that were too new for me to wear she wore for me. Around the kitchen table was mostly where she wore them around. Sure, sure, she wore them into other rooms. I remember listening to her make different sounds with them—scuff-scuffs, and click-clicks, and clip-clops even. Even soft sounds so they sounded no sound was how I heard them. On the linoleum, on the wood, on the tiles, on the carpets were where they were. She wore them everywhere there was to go around our house, and there were plenty of places to go to. We had eight rooms. Eight and a half, if you count the sun porch. But we never counted the sun porch. She never wore them out to the sun porch. "Too dusty," she said.

"Wouldn't want to dust them up before their time," she said. "Wouldn't want to get them too old before they were new."

Then she'd kick a kick, goose a goose step, fling a Highland fling, stomp a stomp—anything to get them going. I remember her picking up a towel and doing the matador. She clicked out triplets with the heels and shouted, "Eh-eh, *toro!*"

I said, "Get serious. This is algebra." And I'd sit at the kitchen table with my books all over it. Pages of paper were scattered for scratch paper with doodles of numbers doodled all over them.

"Why serious? Why not delirious?" she said, and tromped over to where I was so hard that I thought she was going to stomp through the floor.

"Come on," I said.

So she sat. "Let's see," she said. Then she solved it. Then she taught me how to solve it.

"Easy," she said.

"Easy for you," I said.

"Easy for you, too," she said.

Together we packed up my books. She took all the scatters of papers and neatened them up, as she called it. You can imagine it, can't you? Her lining the loose loose-leaf pages so the corners were square to the square, bottoms were flat down flat, sides were straight up straight. "You've got to be neat," she said.

She tapped the papers, tap, tap, tap—like that—on the top of our kitchen table. I swear I can close my eyes today and hear the sound of it.

"Come on," she said. "I need help."

"God helps those who help themselves," I said.

"Set the table," she said.

So I knifed and forked it. So I tossed the plates like I was dealing cards.

"Careful," she said, and she did another triplet.

I put on my horns. Wiggled the tips of my fingers at her. She taunted me with the towel. I charged.

"*Olé!*" she said.

"What about Latin?" I said.

She said, "Later. After dinner."

"No other mother does what you do," I said.

She said, "Baby, this is love." **Q**

Gaz

My father said they all worked in gas. "The same gas they used to use, they still use it now," he said. He said he never bought anything French. He told us not to. How could I afford to on my allowance?

"They use it to cook with," Mother said. "The Mindlins do," she said.

"Gaz?" my sister said. "Gaz? Gaz?"

I liked to hear the sound of her saying it.

"Krup, Krup, Krup, Krup, Krup, Krup, Krup," she said.

I liked to think that Mindlin's mother was someone's father. She had the voice for it. She had the look of it. What a hausfrau, Father said she was, only Mother said that Jews were not hausfraus. "What about the Bonderantes?" I said.

"All the way to hell," my father said. "Ovens," my father said. "The same people still make ovens," he said.

"Who made the Beetle?" I said. "The headlight eyes. The handlebar trunk handle."

"Who do you think made it?" my mother said.

"I don't drink their wine," my father said. "I won't eat in their restaurants. I don't drive their cars. Let me tell you, a Peugeot is crap. Real crap."

Krup, Krup, Krup, Krup, Krup, Krup, Krup.

Krup the coffeemaker. Braun the grinder. Mindlin, Mister Old, Mister Apron-strings, making coffee the way he used to in his kitchen. Me watching him, me retrieving the odd nut that squirted its way away. Me crunching with my teeth, my tongue on the cleaving line that ran down the middle of the bean.

"Bern," my mother would say to my father. "Bernard. Your son's eating off the floor again. Bern."

Krup, Krup, Krup, Krup, Krup, Krup, Krup.

Braun the grinder ground the bean into a fine powder fine

enough for Krup to steam. "Old Mindlin makes a fine cup of coffee," my father would say.

I would not know. My allowance bought me coffee candies that said they were made in Brooklyn.

I loved the smell of grinding. I loved the smell of steaming. I loved to decapitate a wayward bean between my teeth that my father said would end up in the Bonderante tooth pile if I was not careful. "Too many cavities," he said, "to let you keep the gold."

The Braun ground as slowly as an old dentist did. He had that mask, the dentist did, that gas in your face, and you were not laughing, you were not grinning—it was he who grinned.

"Bern," my mother would say to Father. "Bernard. Look how he looks!"

You could hear the particulars. You could think you were hearing the shearing of the middle section, the decapitating of the bean, and then its ping against the sides of the Braun. But no, these sounds were not so singular.

"It's nothing," my father would say. "It's only nitrous."

The Krup was steam, pure steam, sucked by mystery vacuum from one pot of Krup down into the other pot of Krup.

Sister Fran was crawling up to take a swipe at Krup when Mrs. Mindlin shooed her away. Grinding her teeth and shooing, Mrs. Mindlin was. Shooing in a tongue I could not understand.

They took Fran away. She went away, not by Citroën, and when she came back, there was a limp. I did not know the particulars of what must have happened to Fran.

"A simple tonsillectomy," Father said. "Something as simple as a tonsillectomy."

Nothing more.

Why all the shots?

"Why all these shots," I remember my father saying, "when it's tonsils?"

She must have been operated on. She must have been under a sheet. Maybe they shaved her hair. Maybe they used general.

They must have used general in those days. Maybe my father wanted it to be local.

"Incompetents," he called them. "Butchers," he said.

I wonder what they gave for pain. And something to make her sleep. They must have used a mask. Tonsillectomy: sounds like what it is. Means what it is. Siegel in German means Levy, means helper. Medicines in the veins of my helpless sister invading her—like France.

Bonderantes are all around her, swarming over her. Mindlins line the sidelines. Mrs. Mindlin is heading up the nurses in here. Mister mops the floors. The Bonderantes are the high priests, the Mindlins their Levys. There is no audience. No rooting section. No Israelites.

The steam is my sister's breath against the mask.

"This is not a serious operation," the Bonderantes are saying.

I hear no grinding sound the way I would if this were, say, a leg.

"It is almost ready," Mother is saying.

The heat here is percolating like steam against the sides of the Krup.

Did someone say ovens? Did Father say it? Did Sister say it?

"Ovens, ovens, ovens," she said.

She had a Susie Homemaker. It had only the one light bulb. No one ever cleaned it. We made brownies the size of Mother's. I dreamt of slivers of old brownie building up in the back.

Did I wake up one morning from uneasy dreams and find Fran transformed? Written of in another language? What a name for a girl. Crawling the floor like some kind of insect. Oh, it was plain Fran. Zzzzzzzzzzz was the sound of a machine my allowance would not buy.

Like some kind of dung beetle, or locust, was Fran. Depending on the translation. Something that must have had wings and not known it. Something that must have been walking the kitchen floor with legs so small that it would seem to us to be crawling.

Here is what it must have looked like.

Slithering at odd angles.

Avoiding the light.

Secreted under pots.

I thought I saw one resting against a side of the Braun. A spilled bean, it was. Or maybe it was one of my candies.

"Bern," my mother said. "Call in the exterminator!"

Company was coming—the Mindlins, it was going to be—when we found one in Mother's stove, the new self-cleaner heating up to hundreds of degrees and bound to kill off anything alive. Only it was not cleaning. I do not think that it was cleaning—at the time when Fran was limping, almost crawling, snatching up something that had flown from the stove, and then, I swear, making as if to eat it.

Me, of course, I was watching my sister do it as any good brother would do.

"Bern!" Mother screamed, and they grabbed her, the two of them pumping her to free it, what had erupted from the stove.

But surely it was just a bean. A crunchy, slippery, cloven bean, well past its time in the Braun.

Or maybe just a candy. Hey, didn't we see one looking just like a ladybug at the back of Mom's oven? Hey, Fran!

The Braun was grinding, the Krup was steaming. The Mindlins were due over for dinner.

Spanish night at the Siegels'. Nothing fancy. Nothing kosher. No kreplach for sister Fran, who was gagged with a felt gag, sucking her rice from a pap beside the bed while we ate real food in the kitchen.

Rice and beans, I remember it was. I was eating the rice between mountains of the bean. Squishing the rice, I was thumbing it, grinding it, I was squooshing it into a fine powder too fine to lick up.

Mindlin cleaned. Mister, he got on the sterile gloves and soaked the unclean floor with ammonia. Fumes rose from that floor like unseen you-know-whats. You could smell the vapor rising. You could almost see it. But no, no, you could not see it.

"Zyklon," my father said. "It was Zyklon-B."

My father was a chemist. He was *numero uno.*

"Argon," my father said periodically. "Inert."

"Argonne," my mother said. "You never take me anywhere."

"Are gone, are gone, are gone," we said.

"Xenon," my father said. "And Krypton."

"Krypton," I said. "I know Krypton. I love to say Krypton."

"Zyklon," my sister groaned from her room.

It was cold in the kitchen and we were heating ourselves in the heat from the oven. Steam was rising from the Krup like smoke. Smoke was rising in tight circles from my father's mouth until he tossed the cigarette out the window.

He lit another cigarette.

It was dark in the kitchen, and I was watching faces in the glimmers of light.

The grownups were drinking their wine.

I was feeling the table for fallen ash.

Every porch has its stair. The Bonderantes are sitting on our stairs. Why do I think that I can see them from here? Why do I think that I am watching them from sticker bushes? Sticker bushes line the sides of our porch, but am I in them?

Mrs. Mindlin boils water in a pot and throws in handfuls of the grind.

"Why not use the Krup?" my mother says.

Father lights another cigarette.

Mother fans her face.

"Too hot for the time of year," she says.

The doorbell rings.

I dream we are being chased by animals who come at us like wolves on two feet. I know I can talk my way out of anything if only I could talk.

"Liar," someone says. "Another King of the Jews," he says.

My father says, "The effects will wear off."

They chase us to the place where the stairs go down and the

land falls away from us and opens inward. They force us down the stairs. A sign at the bottom says something in that language. It says it in every language.

"The bath," someone says. "It means the bath."

Siegel means lock—or else it means Levy, bringer of wine to high priests.

Which priests?

I am only Marc Siegel. That's Marc with a cee, spelled the way the French spell it.

My sister is plain Fran.

"*Faigel*," my mother says to Fran. "You are my little *faigel*."

Faigel means bird. My sister does not walk. She crawls. The creatures have her by the shank. My sister cannot move.

"Be quick," one of the creatures says.

"Find the brother!" someone says.

"I want Daddy," Fran says. "Where is my daddy?"

The creatures must still be out there. From in here the sounds sound like the sounds of marching. My father tells us to stay seated. My father goes to the window.

From my sticker bush I can see them munching. They are tearing off spears of meat and gnawing to the bone. They are drinking the dark liquid.

"Goink, goink, goink, goink, goink," they slurp. "Kwik, kwik, kwik, kwik, kwik, kwik," they eat.

"You bastards," my father says. "Say the words. Say *Sieg Heil*. Let me hear you say it."

"Bern!" my mother says. "Stop it, Bern," she says.

Does Mrs. Mindlin throw boiling water out the window? No. She does not throw it. But my father. Here comes my father. My father is launching his cigarette. It is flying over the porch and it is landing in one of the bushes.

I can smell the smell of the bush burning.

Watch the sky. **Q**

First Fridays

Mother McNealy was the first person I ever saw dead.

In the quiet of a priest's house made of wood and stone, which absorbed all sound and heat, I saw a woman laid out in a blue dress, candles all around, a portable pew in front of the casket. I was thirteen years old; it was thirteen years ago. I propel naturally toward ceremony and theatrics. I believe I can trace this to my Catholic upbringing. I love a good symbol, even if I have to stretch somewhat to get at it. But I also feel an almost unnatural need to tell the truth after I have lied. Therefore, I must tell you there was another man I once saw dead; it was the pastor of my parish.

Once dead, he was dutifully displayed during all masses around the clock that weekend in February when I was almost eight. Chiefly, I remember that I had on that day a handsome white muff which was not mine, and therefore I loved it so much I took it with me to Communion. I believed myself to be pious, and I enjoyed saying the word to myself—pious, pious—my hands folded inside the muff—pious, pious—as I walked down the aisle, glancing at the waxen man in black, struggling to get the Host unstuck from the roof of my mouth with my tongue.

Being nearly eight, I thought the old pastor ought to be stuffed and propped up all year round in the school lobby, next to the statue of Our Mother Mary. But since I was a person of very little consequence in the parochial grammar school I attended, my idea went unheeded. At that time I still wore the woolen uniform with two strips of material which went up over my breasts, to show that I had none. Then, when I began to get some, the uniform changed to a simple skirt of the same material, so that these developments would not be emphasized.

I was thus de-emphasized at the time of this second death, with my short, ugly blue-and-gray checked skirt and my yellowing blouse. Yet I believed myself to be sacred, holy even, as I walked through the cold hallways of the school, silently and in line with my pious classmates. Sometimes, to draw attention to our piety, we would throw pats of butter onto the ceiling in the cafeteria or knock over the bicycle racks in the parking lot which was our playground. On Fridays, when we clapped the erasers, we always left an eraser mark or two on the side of the building. We were secret vandals, breaking what we could and damaging the unbreakable. We were generally misunderstood. This we accepted as we accepted our grace.

"Do you do this at home?" Sister Facial Scar used to demand, addressing our class as one.

"We don't have bicycle racks at home," some smart aleck would reply.

"Why are you doing this to yourselves?" she asked. "I don't know what you're going to be like when you get older, but it will not be good."

This is a nun; I would expect as much. But you, you I want to make believe we were truly holy. We were not nice, yes. And we were not kind. The worst fears of Christianity seemed to have no hold on us, it is true. But we were holy nevertheless, in the dictionary sense: devout in religion. We couldn't help ourselves; we believed, as children will.

Mother McNealy's death was also the occasion of my first visit to the inside of my pastor's house. It was there that she was laid out in her blue dress and her blue hair. She was beautiful, lying there; so soft-looking, and so cold. Her hair was crimped in little waves around her face, and her hands were folded neatly over her thin, small frame.

Mother McNealy was a woman I knew. She was not a nun, she was the new pastor's mother. Father McNealy, right? I don't know why we called her what we did, but that's how Father spoke of his mother and so that was her name. Once we sang to her in her nursing home, and once I visited her alone, part of a punishment for some folly I can't remember.

When we sang as a group, we sang in the tearoom of her

nursing home. The room was shaped like a bowling alley and had one window in the middle of a long wall. The bottom panels of the room were painted lime-green and above them there was a rose-patterned wallpaper. The carpet was a sort of fake Persian dotted with yet another shade of green. I think once everything had matched, but the colors had faded and now you got this unlikely green triumvirate of color. The effect, when entering the room, was like stepping into the hollow middle of your mother's lime Jell-O mold, bits of fruit around you suspended in congealed mystery.

On the morning we sang, chairs and wheelchairs were lined in three rows along one long wall. Here the members of the home waited. Behind them there was a window, and a day in April, but still not bright enough to light the tearoom. An overhead glass chandelier was lit, as were several standing lamps with fringes. The room looked almost elegant. The room almost came off. But there was the green, and the spittoons. And the inhabitants were all dressed for bed. They waited for us, Mother McNealy among them. There was a smell of scouring; a smell of waiting and counting pulses. We were ushered along the other long wall, and thus we faced the dying.

Sister Facial Scar arranged us boy-girl, with an extra girl at the end, Mary Howard, who looked like a boy anyway. We were also arranged by size; I was in the back line against a paneled wall.

"Come, now, Christine," she said to me. "Don't slouch." I stood up straight and found I could look out of the one window in the room, and this is what I did most of the time we were there, when I wasn't watching Mother McNealy.

"All right, children," Sister said to us gently, as though she liked us, "let's begin with 'Who Threw the Overalls.' Tommy, pitch, please."

We sang.

I think most of us sang to the green carpet or to the rose blossoms rather than to the dying people. Next to me, Mary Eileen Biro sang very loudly. One person who sat in the very last row toward the middle had lipstick, rouge, and eye shadow on but no hair. The light from the window reached her scalp, and spread out upon it. Outside, the sky was very blue, bisected by a bare branch hung from an unseen tree.

The old men and women smiled at us, some nodding their heads to our tempo. We were wonderful shining children for forty-five minutes, singing. We were examples of the faith. It was a scam. We knew this. But we sang.

"Second song, please. Girls only," Sister instructed. "This one is especially for Mother McNealy." Sister turned around for a moment to take one woman's hand. "This is for you, Mother McNealy," she said a bit louder.

"Yes," Mother McNealy replied.

We sang only songs of happiness and life, and we tried not to look anyone in the eye. Mother McNealy sat in the very front, her hands clasped on her lap and her mouth set. She wore bright nail polish and bright lipstick. Sometimes she sang along, in a high, quivering voice, changing pitches if it got too high or too low.

Imagine, a woman who could give birth to a priest.

Sister Facial Scar said, "Now just the boys. Girls, you come in on the second verse."

We sang. When we finished, our audience clapped. Their dry hands made a soft, low patter.

Sister Facial Scar complimented us when we got outside. And Tommy Stanley said, "We do our breast, Sister."

He got five detentions. So did anyone who had laughed.

I didn't like mass, but I liked the church; the atmosphere was so cool, a whisper in darkness. It made me feel there was another world I could slip into if I made the right sign or said the right prayer. As far as I could tell, God had two natures: the hard, all-knowing, fire nature; and the cool, loving, impersonal nature. You know, white statues, porcelain water fountains, a priest's calm stone house, a woman in blue. In what world would I be safe? Which was real? I couldn't tell.

So, kneeling on the cushioned pew with my classmates every week, I prayed rather uncertainly. It never took long. I thought of my sister, locked in her bathroom every night; my mother crying at dinner; my calm, silent father with his perpetually sliding glasses and his books. Once I prayed for Mother McNealy when Father told us she was gravely ill and preparing to meet Christ. Once I licked the wood of the pew in front of me. In the confessional I betrayed my secrets, and prayed for piety. Things began closing in very fast in seventh grade, when we lost our jumpers and began paying attention to a change in pitch. Piety seemed to me the only way for me to get through. But how to achieve it? This involved Mass—and as I've said, I didn't particularly like it. I ran my fingers along the waxed wood, waited for the bells and the incense, and paid no attention to the words.

It was said that if you went to Mass on the nine first Fridays of the month, nine consecutive first Fridays, then you would at least receive the Last Sacraments before you died. It worked like mileage points on frequent air travel. I counted dates, missed Fridays during holidays, started over and counted again.

I am telling you about my childhood.

The second time I saw Mother McNealy I went to her private room in the home. She was too ill to come downstairs. Sister Facial Scar herself dropped me off there after school just to make sure I went, I suppose. She had told me what to sing, and she said that she was going to wait for me in the car in the parking lot outside. It felt strange to be sitting next to her instead of facing her; it was as though I were inside an Egyptian painting, the figures crowded together. This close up, Sister Facial Scar's round eyes looked kind.

"I hope this will give you cause to stop and think," Sister told me as I got out of the car.

A nurse met me at the door.

"How kind of you to come," she said. We took the elevator up—it had wall-to-wall carpeting, literally. And bars all around, for support. Mother McNealy didn't say anything when I came in. She just looked at me and her lipstick twitched a bit, and I took the twitch for a smile.

"I've come to sing to you," I said. "Unless, of course, you'd rather not," I added quickly.

"No, dear, sing," said the nurse, and left the room.

Being alone in Mother McNealy's room was something I had not counted on. We looked at each other for a while, and I wondered if she could still talk or, for that matter, hear. We watched each other, waiting. I was terrified. I thought the old woman might die in front of me, or tell me some secret or vision that I was too young to know. It seemed like we were animals, watching each other like that. So I looked at her clock, at the picture of her son the priest, at her crucifix. When I was through looking at all these things, I looked at the ground. I tried to get God's attention.

"Thank you very much, dear," Mother McNealy told me finally. She had to clear her throat several times before she could get the words out.

In the elevator I thought about the songs I was supposed to have sung as I scratched at a tiny spot of meatloaf sauce on my skirt. What a friend I have in Jesus, I thought. On my fingernail the sauce looked like blood, and I tasted it, just to be sure.

The third time I saw Mother McNealy, she was dead. It was announced over the loudspeaker and there was a hushed silence afterwards, as should be, I think. I could think only in colors: red lipstick, blue hair, yellow pillow, green walls. Then someone sneezed and life began again.

The house, cold and as a priest's house should be, was convenient for death. The body was laid out in the parlor; we were visitors calling. It looked to me as if no one knew quite what to do—we had never done anything like this. Even Tommy Stanley was not brave enough to make the matter lighter than it was.

We lined up before the body. I was somewhere near the back. We took our cue from Sister, who knelt before the corpse, head in clasped palms—so she wouldn't see the body? So she wouldn't smell it? Then each child had a turn in front of Mother McNealy.

When my turn came, I breathed in the perfumed scent of her

body and touched my folded hands to the cool wood of the table on which she lay. It was very quiet. I did not think of tortures in fire or blondes with wings. I saw an old woman's face, with perhaps a touch too much rouge spread on the cheeks. I saw a woman's face as it was when I was in her room with her, silent and thoughtful.

I waited. I could imagine piety, that calm form of holiness, descending upon me. It would be calm and impersonal, neither crazy nor inspired, and it would reform me. Then I would be as distant and cool as God, and just as safely far away. I could imagine it, and I waited for it.

Sister coughed.

Someone belched.

There was a soft exhale of a laugh.

And so I touched my forehead, my heart, and the corners of my shoulders, and rose to go. **Q**

Deliverance

I

Mme Bertrand stood stiff and distracted before him, fist clenched, eye suddenly transfixed by the long ash crumbling at the end of his cigarette. She assured Dr. Flaneur that every door had been locked, every window sealed, shuttered, and curtained shut. She had scrubbed her interior raw with her own two hands, sprayed it with antiseptic, kept out every foreign body, excepting those of medical men, but somehow things just didn't seem clean anymore, "And I can't stand it another second!"

She leapt forward, caught the ash in mid-air, and laid it lengthwise in the ashtray, with neither a break nor burn.

"Well!" said the doctor, impressed at last. Could she please tell him, slowly and from the beginning, how it had all come about?

"Up until a week ago, it was bearable." She paced, tried to sit down, couldn't, and set to wiping out another ashtray with her apron. "Though the chain-smoking was awful. I just couldn't get rid of the *stench*." Her fierce look caused the doctor to snuff out his cigarette. "He just stooped and moped and soon had everyone else stooping and moping about in that unbreathable air. But at least he would still *say* something."

"And what did he say?"

"Oh, it was the same old story, over and over again. He'd point to some pointless thing in his life and then say how pointless it was, how 'incomprehensible,' and when I told him *he* was the only thing incomprehensible, do you know what he said?" She fished a scrap of paper from her apron pouch and read, " 'If only the incomprehension of pointlessness were *not* the beginning of wisdom.' Those were the days, Doctor. Imagine saying such a thing to me. I even heard him say it to the dog!"

"Yes, where is old Rufus?"

"Put down. Where was I? When Bertrand saw I wasn't swallowing any of his incomprehensible nonsense, he took to chanting quietly to himself." She read again, " '*Ego ipse solus sum*'—his very words, Doctor. Bertrand was a Roman Catholic in his youth, and they say those things resurface when you least expect them— withdrawal, sanctuary, monasteries, and vows of silence."

"You must admit it makes sense," interrupted Dr. Flaneur, who took very seriously the Hippocratic injunction of making sense at those crucial moments when there was none. "I suppose he meant something like, 'There's method in his madness.' " But then he thought that Mme Bertrand probably wouldn't have swallowed that one either.

"Makes sense? So tell me how the rest makes sense, too." And she described the days of ominous calm that came with its new terror, a silence broken only by his low, absent-minded whistle as he manipulated some dangerous object. He took to whittling tiny pieces of balsa for hours, with a ten-inch carving knife; he cut articles from the newspaper with abrupt, slashing flicks of the wrist, a razor blade between thumb and forefinger (how she came to regret having hidden the scissors!); he kept cleaning and reassembling the ancient revolver his pappy had left him, clicking the last three bullets like ball bearings, over and over between his fingers. Not that they were in any danger of going off; then again, it might have been better if they had: the noise left her more nervously prostrate than a bullet in the cerebellum.

"Then, three days ago, he cut himself 'accidentally' on an 'accidentally' broken bottle. How white he went," Mme Bertrand reddened at the thought, "and gave me such a look! The sound of running water brought me to my senses, but by the time I reached the bathroom, he had already twisted a face towel around his hand. He glared at me, and without a word went into his 'study.' He hasn't come out since."

"Then it's time somebody went in," concluded the doctor.

As they made their way down the long hall, Mme Bertrand lamented the dirt and disorder—it was all she could do, under the circumstances—but once before the door, she preempted the doctor's poised knocks: Bertrand wouldn't answer. The doctor knocked all the same, for decorum's sake, and waited, his black bag between his hands. Mme Bertrand pushed, and in they went.

Against one wall of a windowless room, partially hidden by the door, Bertrand lay on a sofa, wrapped in a burgundy bathrobe too short for him, tied with a tasseled cord somewhere near the waist. At the end of a pair of lackluster shins flapped two plaid felt slippers, with most of the plaid worn off. He propped his head in one hand, while the bandaged hand lay on its back, fingers half-curled in the air, a dead crab.

Tangled black hair and three days beard made him look grisly enough, but the green luminosity, shed from an opaque glass opening in the ceiling, gave a faint phosphorescent glow to every inch of exposed skin. Mme Bertrand had removed all other sources of light, to prevent electrocution and shadows, where visitors might suspect the lurking of some sickroom unsavoriness. At that hour, the card table before the sofa was still visible.

"Well, Bert, and how are you?" said the doctor, stepping resolutely up to the table, and thrusting forth his hand. Bertrand's bandaged hand made it to the table's edge, where it hung for dear life, time enough for him to smile timidly: the day before he'd knocked out a front tooth by opening the door just when his wife entered. Then the hand fell, caught by the doctor, who shook it vigorously before flipping it over. "Hm. Nasty gash. Now, why would a fellow do a thing like that?"

"I wouldn't know," replied Bertrand, and the low monotone of his voice made it impossible to doubt him. Dr. Flaneur dressed the hand, took its pulse. Bertrand swung himself around to a sitting position, and was thumped, back to front. Meanwhile, Mme Bertrand gently tested with her instep, then pushed Bertrand's chamberpot a little further behind the sofa. There were sighs all around.

"Can I offer you a drink?" Bertrand gestured towards a thermos left discreetly by his wife some time ago, 180-proof pure white alcohol "from fermented prunes," she had said.

"I concur," said the doctor, helping himself generously to a paper cupful. "Excellent aperient. 'Mother Nature's enema,' my grandmother used to call it." He turned to Mme Bertrand and winked. "A wee bit lazy at stool, eh?"

Mme Bertrand nodded, preferring not to go into the details of that particular plan.

"If you don't mind, I think I'll lie down again," Bertrand said to no one in particular.

Sipping his digestive, Dr. Flaneur eyed the papers that covered most of the table before him, but was soon defeated by the disorder. At last, he extracted a page from the piles and said, "So how's the opus coming along?"

Over the page ran a number of ugly little doodles.

"Oh, that. Well," Bertrand looked this way and that, "I've been a little handicapped these last few days . . ." His bandaged hand fell from the sofa to the floor without a thud and lay motionless. No one moved to pick it up. "My heart's not in it."

"Your heart?" whispered Mme Bertrand. "Your heart? If you had a heart—"

"Now, Bertrand," interrupted the doctor, shooing Mme Bertrand further aside. "We all know life's not easy. No one ever said it was, day after day, week after week, month after month, year after year—" and so on, warming himself up to his best professional manner, but in vain: the voice that had penetrated many a sick and lonely heart found not an echo of response in Bertrand's.

"You're all making a lot of useless trouble for yourselves," Bertrand said, to put an end to it. "I've really nothing else to say."

Mme Bertrand and the doctor saw themselves to the door, for Bertrand had rolled his face back into the sofa.

The air of the living room revived them both, and though they had agreed some radical action must be taken immediately, the doctor raised a few professional objections.

"You see, we can't put him away so long as he hasn't *tried* anything. No one would ever take that cut of his for a suicide attempt. He has no conclusive symptoms, he neither smokes nor drinks nor, if I may politely imply . . ." (Mme Bertrand reddened.) "Now, the law is very formal about this. No one gets promoted *felo de se* by talking about it. It's the act that counts. And while it is illegal to kill oneself, unfortunately the law cannot prosecute those who would, until they do. Hm. Medically speaking, of course, suicide is considered an illness, and a mortal one at that . . ." Something in this reasoning distracted the doctor, who muttered to himself, "If only we could somehow provoke—"

"Provoke, indeed!" A voice barged into the doctor's stream of consciousness, followed by the barge himself: Jerry, Mme Bertrand's older brother, brawny and brown with his head on his shoulders and his heart on his sleeve, and further down a fist that spent its evenings more often than not under other people's chins. Having recently received a thirty-page *cri de soeur*, he was in no mood for musings.

"Listen to me. Bertrand mopes, says that nothing means anything, wants asylum, fiddles with guns and knives—so what? All this would make sense if he were in his room right now with a hole in his head. Unfortunately for us all, he's not. Madeleine, have the courtesy to hear me out.

"What are the facts of the matter? Not suicide. There's been no suicide here. Minus the suicide, the facts are simply that his morbid self-pity is driving my sister out of her mind!"

"Well, sir, what do you suggest?" asked the doctor with a skeptical handshake. "Push him out the window?"

"For a start," retorted Jerry, afraid of no man's implications. "Seriously, Doctor, we shouldn't obstruct him—on the contrary! We should give him every possible assistance—"

Mme Bertrand burst into tears.

"And what if he actually succeeded?" rejoined the doctor, speaking for Mme Bertrand.

Jerry was silent on this objection, since deep down inside he didn't consider it an objection at all. On the other hand, he saw no reason for upsetting his sister further.

"He *won't* succeed. He's too much of a worm for that."

"Come, now," said the doctor, "accidents do happen, you know. Bertrand's only human."

"Human, maybe," Jerry replied firmly, "but not a man."

"Man or not," Mme Bertrand broke in, "I want him cured!"

"But he's not sick, I tell you."

"If only he *were*," she sobbed, "I mean, really sick, some awful illness we could all fight together, nurse him back to health, and give him a real reason to live!"

"I think I could manage that," said the doctor abruptly, a strained look on his face. Brother and sister turned of one accord, like a pair of cows mildly aghast at the backfire of Dr. Flaneur's inspiration. The doctor simply nodded as the blood rose up his neck to the tips of his ears. Whether flatus had led to afflatus or vice versa, a sudden sense of relief pervaded the room: a solution had been found. Mme Bertrand said nothing, and Jerry simply remarked that an angel had passed.

"Not Bertrand's, I hope!" laughed the doctor, adding more seriously, "I'll get to work on it right away."

II

All the deadly -ios and -ias that have made modern medicine what it is today were out of the question, even if Dr. Flaneur could induce one of them into a syringe for so humble a purpose as to teach a man a lesson. Besides, the cause required a long drawn-out yet ultimately curable illness; maybe maim him a little, but certainly don't *kill* him—you don't need a doctor for that.

He didn't feel too confident about the more exotic brands, either—the typhoids, malarias, and various paludal bagatelles— partly from medical parochiality, partly from pure patriotism: why look to foreign haunts, when you've got everything you need and more, right here at home?

It still left a good deal to choose from: all kinds of bugs and bacteria pullulate in the very air we breathe, he explained, not to mention lines of unemployed viruses just itching to be sucked into the appropriate syringe and injected into the job. The presence of a woman, and the patient's wife at that, put venereal considerations out of the question. Moreover, Mme Bertrand understandably exercised her female prerogative for dampening the somewhat rampant idealism of her two male counterparts.

"How about giving him a good cold?" she proposed. Jerry and the doctor looked at each other, and eyes rolled.

At last they settled for a blend of the local stuff, nothing too sophisticated—a select choice from among the multitude of maladies yearly spawned by a wonderfully rotten climate and the proximity of an old, oozy river. Though quite proud of himself, the doctor christened it Bertrand's Disease, because he felt a disease invented for the patient should bear the patient's name. As for the eventual serums and such necessary for a cure, he would worry about that later. First things first, and anyway, Bertrand still might manage to do himself in, so why bother?

When the big day came, however, he was alive and lying on his sofa, passive as a fakir on his bed of nails. No mere hypodermic arouses a man who has decided that all intervention is senseless and will neither hasten nor delay the inevitable. Jerry, who attended from the hall at the doctor's request, snickered as if to say, "That's what you think."

Mme Bertrand went white when she saw the needle, the very sight of which pricked her conscience, and a dozen dozing second thoughts leapt to the fore. Her hand lurched out galvanically, but the syringe dived beneath the tourniquet, burying its point into the blue swell. Her knee knocked the night table where the doctor had unpacked his kit, and the phial containing the rest of Bertrand's Disease went spiraling to the floor, where it popped and expired in a tiny yellow puddle.

"What have you done!" cried the doctor, so loudly that Jerry sprung two-fisted into the room.

The question was purely rhetorical, for if anyone knew the extent of the disaster, it was the doctor. He had counted on the remains of his concoction for developing an eventual cure, in case Bertrand's ability to resist proved too weak, a most likely event given his depressive condition. He knew the recipe well enough, but hadn't paid much attention to the proportions. And now, the only hope for controlling the ravages of the disease lay evaporating at his feet, spent by the hand that would have stayed it. He shook his head and said nothing.

Mme Bertrand, too moved to pursue the matter, was ushered out under the burly arm of her brother.

Now the long wait began. As hostess for the siege to save her husband, Mme Bertrand had laid in enough provisions to maintain an army of illnesses. Dr. Flaneur announced it might take anywhere from a week to a month, and though he had a thousand things to do, in a fit of bad conscience offered to stay the first few days. Mme Bertrand had already transformed the whole apartment, now outfitted from kitchen to bathroom, for a fight where each would have his or her job to do.

Jerry, of course, wouldn't hear of leaving; whatever he thought or didn't of the doctor and his methods, experience told him that with odds like three against one, Bertrand didn't have a chance. He insisted on setting up his command post on the couch, where he snoozed and snacked all day and into the night. The doctor installed modern medicine, as best he could, on a camp-bed nearby. As for Mme Bertrand, she was too nervous to sleep.

Perhaps it was the strain, the responsibility, the prospect of a long battle against unknown odds (whatever Jerry thought to the contrary), but all three had felt out of sorts since the day of the inoculation. After twenty-four hours of changing shifts and losing sleep, they began to get irritable. Though Mme Bertrand exhausted herself in the kitchen, not to mention the added tidying up (the doctor turned out, despite his pretensions, to be just as much of a pig as Jerry), the men constantly complained. Jerry had even refused his dinner, tottering from the table on the same old lame excuse, that he didn't feel well at all. Mme Bertrand knew better and took it as a slight; when the doctor tried to explain Jerry's point of view, he got a proper explanation himself, plus tears.

These tears, which should have at least solicited the doctor's sympathy, left him too tired even for exasperation. (Jerry, on the other hand, could die of inanition for all he cared; the doctor considered him an ambulant pile who should have been barred the first day, if only for hygiene's sake.) Weak and indifferent, he almost envied Bertrand, so cozy and peaceful there in his sick bed, maybe his death bed—same difference—resigned to his fate.

In fact, the doctor might have envied him for entirely different reasons—for Bertrand's bizarre reaction to Bertrand's Disease, for instance. No one could have predicted it. Not two hours after the injection, he was wearing a broad, almost angelic grin—so angelic, that for a horrified instant Mme Bertrand thought he was already off to heaven. Before nightfall he sat up, chatting pleasantly with whoever mounted the guard. Color returned to his cheeks, and at noon he even ordered a second helping of chicken broth.

"Couldn't you put some steak in it?" he asked, his little joke to raise morale.

No one laughed, no one even seemed to notice. The three valiant nurses were too wrapped up in their own health problems, psychological, psychosomatical or, a mere forty-eight hours later, even physical.

For example, the good doctor had broken out in a rash that did more than itch; rufescent crusts, then scabs formed overnight, their livid halos spreading from his face down to his ankles. Jerry developed a wide anthrax at the base of his neck, with a swelling beneath the armpits that promised more to come. As for Mme Bertrand, discretion demands a more circumspect account, especially considering her mental state, which degenerated exponentially in relation to her efforts, far and beyond the call of failing capabilities, to keep things tidy.

None of them knew anymore exactly how, much less why, they went through the motions of nursing, when obviously *they*, not Bertrand, were in need of care. The doctor took showers all day, Jerry no longer had the courage to leave his couch, and Mme Bertrand dozed uneasily the entire afternoon in the chair, originally meant for vigils, next to Bertrand's sofa. Each had secretly— or not so secretly—wished Bertrand was dead at one time or another, but that's only human nature; now, all three felt so awful, they half-wished themselves dead, which is human nature, too.

For Mme Bertrand, it was more than half a wish. Humiliated by disease and housekeeping difficiencies, she desired more and more each day to be her last. She left the sick room only to fetch between-meal snacks for Bertrand, and otherwise languished in her chair.

Meanwhile, Bertrand's complexion went from recovery-red to in-the-pink. After a while, he decided he wanted a shave, and she agreed feebly to hold the mirror for him as he dipped into a small oval wash basin filled with hot water. Each stroke of the razor discovered a rosy glow which beamed through the thick, stiff hedges of lather flecked with black molt. Mme Bertrand watched on, steadying herself against the wash basin as much as she steadied it, a perilous way of keeping her balance that soon had her swaying gently. Bertrand caught the basin as she swooned. The mirror shattered.

Despite the clatter and bang, neither of the men down the hall budged, and so Bertrand dragged her as best he could onto the sofa. Not knowing what else to do, he wandered out of his room, down the hall towards the living room, whistling softly all the way.

The sight he saw just before the living room door cut his whistle short. Though feeling fitter than ever, he hesitated, doubting his resurgent senses because—you never know, it might just be some last, sickly mirage.

Dropping to one knee, he wetted his forefinger, touched the spot of ash, and brought it to his tongue, then spit: the ash was real, all right, and so was the ashtray, face down on a very spotty carpet. The event troubled him a little, jarring as it did with certain memories. He shook his head and, still on his knees, peered cautiously around the corner into the living room.

A fried egg eyed him askant from a cracked plate not three feet away, while its twin, burst like a spleen by a corner of burnt toast, still clinging, ran its plastic dribble off the edge. On another plate, something swam in a pale juice, fork at half-mast in a mound of instant potatoes, next to a glass of what looked like lavender Coca-Cola. On the couch, surrounded by more of the same, sat the doctor and Jerry.

Jerry rasped and caught his breath, his eyes bulged at Bertrand, but his mouth simply hung open, thick-lipped and speckled. As for the doctor, he didn't even turn his head, but gazed into some infinite distance about two feet in front of him, his chin on his chest. Before them spread, like the little anarchy of a chess game disrupted by the arrival of some clumsy third party, a many-leveled array of medical bottles, some capped, some open, some upright, some on their sides, even a few upside down. There was also a half-used syringe. Bertrand could see blood, like a tiny intestine, unraveling in some livid liquid, and a violet-tinted drinking glass, caked at the brim.

"My God," Bertrand muttered and looked discreetly away, a little disgusted, to tell the truth. The offending took no offense: falling to pieces apparently called for all their concentration.

Bertrand tiptoed away to the bathroom, where he showered a good twenty minutes before abruptly silencing both faucets—he could have sworn someone had rung downstairs. After a short struggle with his shoes, he hustled into an overcoat and headed down the stairs, grouped in hurdles of two and three.

The transom window beamed benevolently on Bertrand as he tugged with both hands at the massive street door. It swept slowly and widely open, a rose light filling its frame in a perfectly fitted tablet, as if God Himself were about to speak—but didn't, of course, and left Bertrand instead blinking blindly at the foot of His second creation: Dawn. **Q**

Penance

I was standing on a street corner when two people (call them A and B) approached. "Give us money," they said, and cut me with knives. "Never," I said, and ran away.

Another day, I was dining in a fine restaurant; A and B sat down at my table, this time accompanied by C. "We'll kill you," they said, and showed me the gun. "I won't negotiate," I said. I got up and left the restaurant, whistling.

On a different occasion, I was accosted by D, who is a friend of A's, and is known also, I believe, to B and C. "You will suffer," said D, and he showed me pictures of the pain that awaited me. I laughed in his face, and went to buy stamps. I sent a letter to the editor, one to the Pope, and one to Mollie Katzen, who wrote the Moosewood cookbook. None of them wrote back.

I thought to myself, I have failed here, somehow, it seems.

I spent long hours in dark places; I gave to charity; I fasted. Slowly, I grew old; eventually I died. A and B, crafty in their old age, came and released snakes into my open grave. **Q**

Withholding

"I have a secret," she said.

"Not interested," he lied.

She undid her hair and shook it down around her shoulders. He started going through her desk.

"It's not in there," she said. She set about brushing her hair.

"Doesn't matter," he said.

He pulled the drawers out of her dresser and clawed through her underwear. He searched in her closet, under her bed.

"It's not something you can find," she said.

"Shut up," he said. He grabbed her wrist and yanked her off the bed. He felt in her pockets, then tore her clothes off.

"You'll never know," she said. "You'll never understand."

"Shut up," he said. "Shut the fuck up." **Q**

A Descent, in the Company of a Pig

She happens to be falling. The pig is still with her, nestled comfortably in her arms. "Our destinies are intertwined," she says softly. The pig looks at her, snorts, and looks away. "Oh, pig," she says, "do you love me still?"

The pig, indifferent, watches the moving shapes far below. **Q**

A Brief History of Male Nudes in America

They step from behind my mother's shower curtain, pose like acrobats, like soldiers. They lie bound in the afternoon light of the downstairs bedroom. There are buttons on the floor. Someone's wallet on the dresser. On the back of a chair, a shirt leaves everything to the imagination. It is a workshirt with the smell of hay still in it. It's khaki, short-sleeved, long-sleeved, on the back *Sugarloaf Bowl* machine-embroidered with *Del Rio* below it.

I have my eyes open. I see them strut. I see them scurry from the bathroom back to my mother's bed, their big white backsides haunting our household like bad winter colds.

My mother is divorced and entertains at odd hours.

I get home from school and on the kitchen counter she has a peanut butter sandwich for me or Hostess Snowballs, raisins, applesauce, or a Mars Bar. At the bottom of her closed bedroom door there is a crack of light that exhibits the depths to which we all will fall.

Karl Winckelman's truck is parked out front. My mother's Talbott bedspread is probably folded back, in thirds, to the end of her bed, where it is a silky white margin my mother tells Karl Winckelman to keep his feet off. By four o'clock, they are standing in the kitchen asking me about homework.

"Hey, kiddo," Karl says, "I have a way of multiplying with my fingers."

My mother does not mind discussing her life with me—an only child, a girl already taller than her mother. She explains sex as biology by candlelight. She describes her need and desire as electric impulses that are strong enough to roll a rock uphill. She characterizes her love of men as something that happened to her in the cradle when her mother's back went bad and it was her daddy that held her against his chest and in his hands.

"Hey, nothing in this life is perfect," my mother says.

They work up appetites at our house—man-sized. Cans of tuna, a dozen eggs, a red onion sliced thick. I have seen these men make sandwiches I could not get my hands around.

My mother stands off to the side, sweet in a brocade robe or sexy in a yellow T-shirt, and watches, sometimes showing them where the crackers are.

Karl Winckelman asks me if I have finished my homework. Barry Rivers asks me where I got my green eyes from. Tim French asks me if there are any more clean towels. Some Cuban guy asks me if our dog bites.

Boy cupids, men of stone, athletes, bathers—they kiss and fondle my mother, then give me a sidelong look. "This is April," she tells them in the way of an introduction. "She's on the honor roll. In the choir. You can't slip anything by her. Don't even try."

At the top of the stairs or in the kitchen doorway, I am where I can see it all. They step out of their clothes or my mother undresses them, and in the golden light of the Nile, they are the bare figures of love and promise. In my mother's care, they see themselves twice their real size, agile, long-limbed, generous, hung like bulls, sweet as new fathers. They are fast to sleep and slow to awaken. She tiptoes out of her room in the mornings and puts her finger to her lips, and our world is safe again, or maybe isn't. **Q**

Services

Stand right here, son. Here they come. This should not take long. We can do something later. Grandpa would be proud of you. Shake hands with a steady grip. What would you like to do? Look the person in the eye. We can take the car. Here comes Mr. White. You could ask a friend. Mr. White knew Grandpa when the two of them were boys. Want to see a movie? Speak up loud enough. How about the Skyride? Please stand up good and straight. I could take some time off. Always say the person's name. Hello, Mr. Beck, this is my son. We could camp out. Grandpa worked with Mr. Beck. We could go to the lake. Look at all the flowers. Where did we put the tent? Listen to what people say. Where are the fishing poles? People shake hands when they come and shake hands when they go. Would you like a puppy? I have got the tackle box. Do like I do, son. Hold still—your hair is all uncombed. His eyes were wide open. Here comes Mrs. Ross. I was talking to him. We could go out West. She might want to hug you. He could not talk to me. We could climb up to the snow. I had his hand. Sometimes women hug instead of shaking like we do. I could talk to them at school. His hand did not move. I see some more people. There was nothing they could do. Here—let me fix your tie. It does not even look like him. What should we do first? They are saying such nice things. We have time to do them all.

Stand here beside me, son. **Q**

Emergency

Are you here all by yourself? Does it hurt right now? Here—this seat is empty. Can you think of other things?

Did you grow up here in town? Have you seen the nurse? We live within walking distance. Have you got a dog? Did you go to First Street School? Let me hold your coat. Did you have Miss Wright? Look! They are bringing someone in. It is just Calhoun and I. How well do you sleep? Are you sure about Miss Wright? Did you go to the lake? He is getting oxygen! Did they throw you in? That must be the wife. Did you climb the cliff? Have your children moved away? Do you have Blue Cross? Did she keep you after school? That could be a heart attack! Did your father take you hiking? Were you drafted? So was I. Do you still have your bike? Did you go to First Street School? My name is Dick. Here comes the doctor! Do you go to work? Did you ever see Miss Wright without her glasses on? Were you taller than your father? That must be the son. This is where we brought him. Did they just call your name? My son lives out West. Is there someone you should call? I will wait out here.

Did you go to First Street School? **Q**

What to Do Today

This is the list for today. Bandit got away. Yesterday is not done yet. My wife does not feel good.

He got underneath the fence. Take the porch screens down. My son is out West somewhere. Cut firewood. Look for Bandit. Wash the windows. The mail has not come. Fill the hole that Bandit dug. Check the cellar door. Have you seen a spotted dog? Fix the kitchen light. Bandit likes the Mighty Dog Pure Beef and Gravy Mix. Do the grass. Pick up the paper. Ask the mailman, too. Sometimes Bandit disappears for two weeks at a time. Change the oil. My son is single. Wash the pickup truck. Bandit might have crossed the highway. Pay the water bill. Buy a longer leash for Bandit. Find the grocery list. There could be a bitch in heat. Pick up postage stamps. Set the clock for six A.M. My wife is upstairs. Bandit is allowed inside but not up on the bed. My son left things in his room. Wash out Bandit's bowl. Get my wife's prescription filled. Sweep the front porch off. What a good he-dog he is. Clean the gutters out. We are almost the same age, going by dog years. My son travels. Find the leak. Finish yesterday.

My wife says, "Let's get Bandit fixed."

Put out a bowl of Mighty Dog. **Q**

It Helps to Write Things Down Like This

My brother likes a girl. We are meant to be asleep. Pooch gets out sometimes. I write things down at night.

The girl my brother likes is May. This is Grandma's house. I write underneath the covers. Pooch sleeps on the bed. I see by the flashlight. We go to Sunday School. Grandma stops outside our door. Pooch is all grown up. May sits near the front. We take cod liver oil. Pooch slips his collar off. I see my brother watching her. Pooch runs away. We wash our hands. May's mother drives a car. We can get up from the table when our plates are clean. Pooch does not come back for days. May's father lives at home. You should see the words that they write on the boys' room wall. I saw May with earrings on. Pooch comes back skin and bone. I practice on the instrument from five to six P.M. We get an allowance. My homework is not done. Grandma puts clean underwear out for us every day. Pooch gulps his chow. He rolls in pooh. May's mother wears makeup. Pooch lies right in front of us and licks himself down there. Grandma puts fresh sheets on. Our milk is pasteurized. We say, "Let's get Pooch a wife." Miss Wright might call on me. Grandma says one is enough. Pooch does everything. They say a boy who touched himself grew warts and went insane. This light needs new batteries. May says hello to me.

Good night, May.

I love you. **Q**

DIANE WILLIAMS

The Fuck

The pungency, the mystery, the awesomeness of his idea was terrific. Mother of God—he actually had a cloth and a spray bottle of something, because he was dusting his truck. His truck was blocking up our street that we live on.

As I ran away from him, I shouted, "I am not trying to run away from you!" Brutally, I kicked what I decided was my own stone, and I found a limp walking stick—a dead tree branch, smooth, just the right height—after it was boring for me to be brutal.

Ferocious, hateful dogs, working as a team, barked at me.

What are the Williamses putting that up for? I wondered, when I turned my corner. Now, he was over there, in their yard, not looking at what he was doing with their swing set, speaking only to me, when I came along.

There was no mention of being ill or an illness mentioned which was of an extreme or of a debilitating nature. Pleasure was the centerpoint, sexual pleasure, fun, surprise, gamey delight—seldom, well, all right, *once!* disgust. He did not express desire other than sexual, which he was confident he would gratify soon. He had no concern that any woman, man, girl, or boy would not be a good enough provider for him, or could somehow disappoint him, or turn up incompetent. Beauty, intelligence, education, gentility, cleanliness, worldly success, a moral attitude—none of these was a standard he ever referred back to. Salesmanship was stressed. No sense of loss, never sorely missing anyone, no concern over betrayal, no money problem was expressed, and yet, even so, I behaved curtly. I behaved as if he had digressed. **Q**

The Guider of the Prick

She wanted Bill to obey her. She wanted that very much. When Bill came down out of the tree, his mother was a little afraid of him, but she said, "Good"—meaning, she was glad that he was back down.

Boy, she thought, is Bill ever a handsome boy. She flung her arms around Bill. Then she tested the skin on her own arm with her fingertips to see if it was still as soft as silk, and it was.

Would Bill's mother ever say to Bill, "You've done enough for me already?"

Bill gets angry now, as a grown man, when some woman guides his prick for its entry into her cunt hole.

But back to when Bill was the pluckiest little boy in the world, sitting on a tree branch, and his mother had thrown a small rock at Bill, and his mother wept and Bill wept too. Bill saw apology, sadness, and disbelief in his mother's face. In Bill's face, his mother saw ordinary crying going on.

This is what Bill looks like as of today: He is large and unkempt, with unruly dark hair and dark eyes. His mother is proud of him. He is the keeper of the flame. **Q**

The Revenge

She sat in a chair and looked out a window to think sad thoughts and to weep. Everything she saw out the window was either richly gleaming or glittering, owing to a supernatural effect. But she was not unused to this. She unlocked the front door. An infinitude of catastrophes was, as usual, apace—even as she walked out to the road. The ground was mushy from a recent rain. Her mind was not changing. Her mind had not changed in years. Somebody's headlights were blinding her. Her idea of a pilgrimage or of a promenade excited her. She was stalking, going swiftly down the avenue. She arrives at a plausible solution for at least eight percent of her woes. I know what she is thinking and am envious of her. But I am shitting on it. **Q**

In My Mother's House

The crowd comes at night while I am sitting on the sofa, sleepwalking—or, I suppose, sleepsitting, you could say. Mother shakes my shoulders, says, "Straighten your eyebrows, pussy." I see the men moving in the room. I see the men emptying their pockets, taking off their wristwatches, their coats, their things. They are making adjustments. I see the stage lit up over there, on the far side of the room.

Mother tells me to stand up. She uses tape to tape my thing up so I will sing in a higher tessitura, which is prettier, she says. Mother says I am her singing girl. She says my singing will shatter glass, and wake the dead, and break hearts. She says all of these men have come here to hear me sing.

I move my feet apart and I am bending my legs so Mother can get my thing taped up up into my crack.

"Sissy, crouch down a little lower, honey," Mother says.

Mother and one of the men are doing it on the sofa.

I am chatting with some of the fellows about the durability of railroad spikes and ties; the character of the minor, as opposed to the major, mode; the meaning of the dream I think I am still having.

My brother is cleaning mobile homes in Alabama.

I offer libation to the men Mother and I are entertaining. I have a tray with glasses of iced tea on it and a box of imported pastries.

I have my hands.

I have my mouth.

I have my body, my youth, my life.

I have a niece, born months early by Caesarean section whereby the mother's abdominal and uterine walls are cut through: Caesar was supposedly born thus.

Anyway, the men take the iced tea off my tray and from time to time take a cookie.

I have seen these men throw glasses through glass and carry women across thresholds. I have seen these men being men from Ohio and getting old. I have seen the strength of men. I have seen their cocks and how they move them. I am the son of several different husbands.

The tape Mother uses is most reliable. The stage is a jerry-built affair. The iced tea is just the thing, as are the cookies, though they are not really imported. Nothing we have is imported, except, I suppose, the men, who are mostly, I think, from Bulgaria.

We live here at 134 1/2 South Front Street. We listen to music on the radio, Mother and I do. Sometimes we dance. I am only recently a singing girl.

Have all of these fellows been here before?

I wish I could sing higher when I sing and talk more perspicaciously when I talk and serve more gracefully when I serve the things I have to give.

Mother says, "Breathe, darling, breathe!"

My father says that railroad spikes rust and railroad ties split, that the minor mode is not necessarily more melancholy than the major, that my dream is not a dream, properly speaking. My father says I am not a singing girl, that the stage is not a stage, that my mother is not my mother. He asks after my brother and takes another cookie and queries me on cleaning materials.

I put my hand on my father's cool, white chest. I let go of the tray and give him a perfect, sweet, hopeful blowjob. He comes in my mouth, moaning the word "Alabama."

"Bunny," Mother says. "Come here, bunny, and let some of these fellows get a look at you," she says. "Show them your putzie, honeybunch," Mother says. "Bend over and give them a little look."

Mother says, "Thou wert the goodliest knight that ever man hast seen, and the truest that ever hast a woman loved."

One of the men hits Mother's face. He says, "I'll hit you again." He says, "Do you want me to hit you again?" He hits her again.

These men tell the grandest tales of sea and air. They sometimes take me driving with them in their trucks. Sometimes we stop and they put a hand on my body and squeeze.

Mother is tied to the spreader. The fellows are asking her where she wants them to put things inside her. She answers with immense politeness.

The men are pouring iced tea on her. They are talking in their native language.

"Mother," I say. "Yoo-hoo, Mother," I say. "Telephone," I say. "Someone's at the door," I say. "Delivery," I say. "Hey," I say. "Hey, Mom."

"Now, sweetheart," Mother says, "come to the stage with me and show them your stuff."

"Pumpkin," Mother says. "Baby doll," she says, "come." "Come on up here and break a leg," one of the fellows says.

Mother is in her underwear—her panties and her brassiere. "Mom," I say, "what is libation?"

"Where is Bulgaria?"

"What is a knight?"

"Where is Alabama?"

"Who is Caesar?"

"Where is the sea?"

"What is a mobile home?"

A Western Union boy comes to the door with a telegram from my brother. It says: "If P equals 1 means P is true, and P means that P is asserted, then the concept of assertion is furnished twice, once by the interpretation of P, and once by the explicit statement P equals 1."

My father unties Mother from the spreader and lays her out on the stage. Mother manages a whispered "Thank you." Father holds her legs in the air and moves his body to and away from Mother. "Please," Mother says. The crowd of men gathers around to listen. "If it would be no trouble," Mother says. "I would very much appreciate it," she says. "If you please."

There is a man in the house wearing a suit, who is punching his hand with his other hand, again and again, punching his hand, punching his hand, with his fist, the fist he has made with one of his hands. I could watch the man punch his fist. But do I? Do I watch? Do I give even the fleetingest consideration to the thought that here is something to see? Do I listen? Do I learn?

The Western Union boy observes Mother on the spreader. "Tighter," he says to the man operating the machine. "Wider," he says. "Longer." "Farther."

He makes the necessary adjustments and then, with his hands and his mouth and his life, takes Mother hard, up the ass. I hear Mother moaning a word I have never heard.

The imported men talk among themselves of places, jobs, qualities of things. I see them watching the action without facing that way. I see their cocks coming alive once again. I smile to myself and go for more iced tea. On my way out of the room, I see the telegram from my brother. I pick it up and read it several times. What would this sound like as a song? I wonder. To what kind of music would this text be set?

The Western Union boy says my father is not my father. He says my brother is correct in his thinking. He says he is going to meet my brother in a clean mobile home in Alabama.

The Western Union boy is very handsome, but none of us has yet to see his cock. When, Mother wants to know, will we see his chest? Is it white and smooth? And will he come, Mother wonders, in my mouth? Will he stay, Mother wonders, for the show?

Oh, how could I raise my tessitura? How could I sing more prettily than I can sing?

"Darling," Mother says, "this whole big bunch of men has come over here just to get a little listen to your pretty singing they've been hearing so much about. You know how people love to hear you sing, lamb chop. You are Mommy's little singing girl, aren't you? Aren't you the little singing sensation? Don't you sing just as high as any old woman you ever heard? Now, dumpling, please. You don't want these nice men to go away empty-handed, do you? You'll at least sing one silly little old Italian aria, won't you? We already got you all taped up, chipmunk. I can't even see your little thing at all, I got it taped up in there so nice. Now, angel, please, come on in here and give these nice men a little sample of your show. Just let these fellows get a chance to hear how high my little baby doll can sing when he wants to sing high notes."

The Western Union boy, with his hands and his life and his assertions and his telegram and his iced tea and his imported cock, fucks all of the men.

I have heard that there is a place in Mexico with green water and white sky. Foreign men have great adventures there, sailing the green sea, singing Italian arias, breaking the hearts of women, dancing. Nothing in Mexico, I have heard, is imported. The music is all in the major mode, boys do not sleepwalk sitting up, mothers wear their clothes, and fathers are fathers.

I am my mother's sleeping, singing girl. I have a brother in Alabama. My mother is here with me in our house, screwing the Western Union boy. My thing is taped up in my crack. I live at 134 1/2 South Front Street.

I want to swim in the water of Mexico, under the white sky.

I straighten my eyebrows with the tip of a finger and I go for more iced tea.

Mother turns on the radio and we dance to a song in the minor mode. The Western Union boy tells the men he is going to ask my brother about railroad spikes and ties. "They have been known to last," he says, "almost nearly forever." The men vent their disagreement, which provokes an episode of violence. Blood is shed, lives are lost, bodies are thrown out the window.

Mother and I keep dancing to a song that is not, properly speaking, melancholy.

"Mom," I say, "what is assertion?"

"What is interpretation?"

"Where is Mexico?"

I am still sleepwalking. Or -sitting.

It turns out we are out of iced tea and we are out of imported pastries. It is my job to go get more. But where? Where does one go to get iced tea and imported pastries at night, or anytime, in a small town in Ohio?

I go out. I mount my bicycle and ride it. I go through red lights without stopping. I ride for many days and many nights until I see a sign advertising exotic teas and desserts. I buy green tea and Italian cakes. I ride back to Ohio, singing Bulgarian folk songs, thinking of the crowd of men at home, and of their cocks and how they move them.

I am still naked, riding my bicycle, singing Bulgarian folk songs, and my thing is still taped up in my crack, so my tessitura is high, which is pretty, and my singing must be waking the dead. There is no glass to shatter nor hearts to break.

There is a mobile home in the room and the carpet is covered with green tea and cookie crumbs. Mother and the men are dancing—they pick up their feet and then bring their feet down onto the carpet. The tea and cookie crumbs fly up from the carpet and stick to Mother and to the men. They dance faster and faster until they have green tea and cookie crumbs on their bodies and until they are making noises I can hear even with the loud music coming from the radio, and then they fall down onto what tea and cookie crumbs are still left on the carpet and not on their bodies, onto the carpet. The music, in the major mode, keeps playing on the radio.

I watch the dancing from a window of the mobile home.

I applaud and whistle and cheer.

"*Bravo!*" I say.

"*Ura!*"

"*Olé!*"

The men gather outside the mobile home and call to me through the window. They want me to sing.

One of the men comes into the mobile home. He grabs me. He says, "Do you know the one Rosa Ponselle used to do?" He lashes me with the rope he is holding. "Do you?" he says. He hits me in the face, on the chest, on the backside, with the little rope.

I loose myself from the man. I put a hand on his arm and squeeze. "Darling," I say to him. I sip my iced tea. I straighten my eyebrows. "Sweetheart," I say.

I look out the window to Mother. I see her adjust her brassiere, cross her legs, fix her hair with her fingertips. She looks over at me, waves, smiles.

I wave back, smiling, to Mother.

The Western Union boy perspicaciously says that modes have been known to rust and to split, sofas to break hearts and to dance, that my brother is not in Alabama, that libation is a folk song, that sleepwalking is not necessarily melancholy, nor a dream an assertion. He says that I am not, properly speaking, the son of all of these men.

"Hey," I say. "Give me a break. Cut us all some slack, huh? Ease up a little. Relax. Take it easy. Sit back in your seat, man.

Take a breather. Let go a little, huh? Enjoy yourself. Take some
R & R. Get some rest and relaxation.
  "Come on, man," I say. "Just give us a little peek, huh?"

  I want to go off with these big men and have some
adventures with them at sea, on land, wherever. I want to drive a
truck with an arm around one of these fuck-hard lovers. I want to
fuck one of them.
  I want to be one of them, fucking me.
  I want to be one of them, fucking Mother.
  "Mother," I say.
  "Yoo-hoo, Mother."

  A man comes into our house—he tears the screen door
off its hinges, breaks the glass of the larger door. His hand is
wrapped in something. He says he is a contractor, here to solve
problems. He says I owe someone something and that he has come
to get it. He says he has a certain caliber pistol in his wrapped
hand. He has something wrong with his lip—I want to reach out
and touch it, rub it, make it better. But he jumps back and waves
his wrapped hand. I introduce him to Mother. "This is my
mother," I say. "What is it that you want?" I say. Other men come
forward, offer to assist this man in the getting of what he has come
to get.

  Hey, whatever happened to that young, good-looking
Western Union boy? Did we ever satisfy our curiosities about him?
Did we see his cock? Did we fuck him? Did he fuck us? Did he fuck
Mother? Was he gentle? Was he true? Could he sing?

  My father must be my father. We have certain traits in
common. Our hands, our mouths, our lives—they are similar.

  The men take glasses of iced tea off the tray I am holding
and, from time to time, throw the glasses through the window near

the stage. Mother, in her underwear, picks up the broken glass in the room, cutting her hands and bleeding on the carpet.

Mother says, "Call the police!" She says, "Get the neighbors! Run to safety! Lock the doors! Hide the silver!" She says, "Forgive me. Please pardon me. I am so sorry. Please," she says, "all of you—please forgive me."

She says, "I wake up at night and cannot catch my breath."

The blood from Mother's hands is on the window, the stage, the sofa, the carpet, the mobile home, the ceiling, the walls, her body. The blood has got in her hair. "What a mess," she says.

"Crumb cake," she says, "why don't you turn on the radio?"

The contractor comes back. "Hey," he says, "you know that woman? She was fake," he says. "I don't know what you did, but she was no good," he says.

"Well," I say, "how about if I sing for you?" I say. "Major mode or minor?"

I want to apprehend the meaning of my brother's telegram. I want to sing an Italian aria about the durability of railroad spikes and ties for the pleasure of my mother. I want my father to be my father. I want my eyebrows to lie forever straight and my thing to be forever taped up into my crack. I want to know the secret of the man in the suit, the one punching his hand, the one, I see now, who has disappeared.

I want to swim from the waters of Mexico to Bulgaria, to a new crowd of men, to new dead to wake, new hearts to break. **Q**

Bedtime Stories

His name was Rimbaud—not the poet, but the scowler. She had been blind since birth, but did not mind. Darkness could be a shelter.

Some people were learning Spanish. Others were struggling with German. A lucky few were learning Udius, a language that had never existed.

He had written so much during his lifetime that he had lost track of his life.

Every time he slipped into his wife's pink slippers, he felt he was sliding into an abyss.

When he walked the busy sidewalks, he often wondered why the people who walked the same sidewalks seldom smiled. Years later he lost interest in the question, and also seldom smiled.

The penniless woman sat down on a bench and opened her legs to let in the summer breeze. When she walked away, the air smelled of broken promises.

The automobile crash was so eye-grabbing that all the passersby were jealous of the victims.

When he picked up the quarter, he thought he was picking up the remains of his life.

Jane, famished for love and caring, went to a stranger's garden and pulled out six white roses, which she ate while weeping. Then she returned to her husband's house, spacious and well-lit, and ate him too.

The mongrel woke up one last time and growled at the darkness, hungry for more news.

Her bra held all her boyfriend's fantasies. Is it any wonder he winced in shame every time he undressed her?

The rainstorm was three days old. No one in the village wanted to know it was three days old. Two days later, it turned into a snowstorm. Everyone was much happier.

Classical music was his first love. His second was stuffing dolls with newspapers soaked in bowls of sour milk.

The orange he was peeling with his hands was green, but this only made him feel he was the luckiest man alive. He was still a young man, and the orange was his first one.

He would read books all day, and burn them at night; he wanted to stay warm and that is why he burned the books.

Go up the hill, he told his wife. She did.

Sing me a song, the clown said to the captive audience. They did—but not before putting up a long and bitter struggle.

His name was Judas—like his treachery.

For his birthday, his wife had bought him a robot woman, who could do all that he wished. But he made her take it back.

Transfiguration was a word beyond his comprehension. He was a simple man, like his savior.

. . .

His wife showed more and more of herself. Her husband liked this. One day she realized there was nothing left to show; that he had seen it all.

An automobile is a beautiful thing, but not as beautiful as a woman sipping coffee, in a café, in Paris, on an autumn day, with a writer nearby, writing a story about a woman sipping coffee, in a café, in Paris. **Q**

Two Cheers for Enjambment

                    w-

here   here

The Dead Fathers

Have you noticed how the dead fathers
give themselves to poems?

They do as they're told
as if print had the power

to transform them into children.
Barely awake now, they lean into mirrors

fogged from the shower,
tying their ties there,

parting their hair, patting their faces
with alcohol.

Outside, the sky glows in the east.
Lights are blinking on in the windows of small presses.

Clocks are ticking the libraries awake,
the bookstores.

Slowly, smelling of talcum
and lather, the dead fathers

sip the last of their coffee,
shut briefcases crammed

with unfinished business,
and step from their houses into metaphor.

Head

the man took
a look at me
then he went
at it (I did
not mind one
bit) so used
to hard work

Wired

She had a knack for licking
metallic objects—fishhooks,
boot buckles, garbage cans.

Water was her enemy, kissing
everything she loved into rust.

Though men in white coats came
from across the country, no one
would stand behind the glass.

Dark Square

We will all die dreaming
something of this world:
its eggs, its dust, feathers,
body of bread.
It is late, moonless,
the whole house sways with sleep.
A sleek marlin
wavers toward the Mexican sun.
High-voiced children pass
through the graveyard gates,
carrying little pines.

Minnows

Looking down
into a pool
of clear water,
I see
flakes of light.
Black robes
that have dropped
to the bottom.

Among them,
I am very
careful.

For Mad Prospero They Stand Still

Prospero can open their hearts
with his mouth. Them
not realizing he uses teeth.
Them then with open
chests. It was these ignorant
bitches built the world,
losing their bellies of it.
Prospero does his part, sure.
Listen: It's work. Everybody
knows it.

Acoustically Sound

Apollonius of Rhodes. Geronimo.
Galileo Galilei. Lady Jane Grey.
Mad Anthony Wayne. Maximilian.
Napoleon Bonaparte. Dirk Strikker.
Zelda Fitzgerald. Basil Mumma.
Samuel Maverick. Friedrich Nietzsche.
Francis of Assisi. Leon Trotsky.
Nicolaus Copernicus. Billy the Kid.

Revising Shakespeare

I don't want to be a father.
I don't want to die.

Consecration

She said—God, Michael.
Then—Michael, God.
As if it were an introduction
or she communion.

Seven Natural Wonders

The Grand Canyon, Arizona.
Rio de Janeiro Harbor,
as approached from the sea, Brazil.
Iguassu Falls, Argentina.
Mt. Everest, Tibet and Nepal.
The Nile River, Egypt.
The Northern Lights, the Universe.
Pamela Lentine, Oak Park, Illinois.

What She Saw

Looking down into the bowl,
she saw that she had passed
a long thin sliver
of something—
a bit of meat, perhaps,
or a peeling from a fruit,
mottled and scaly.
She watched it float,
take on water, swell,
until what she saw
was a salmon
that had dropped
its final tumorous roe
in some distant valley
of her body,
and then drifted
with the tide
downstream to her delta,
out into her yellow sea.

Counterpoint

There is a little
black spot
on this piece of
paper.

I do not
expect you
to understand.

Burial Plot

Kill me
so my body
can dangle
on your crucifix
between your holy
breasts

The Core

It was all smelly
and yellow
and used-up
and he didn't want it
anymore
he said
open your hand
take it
as if I would know
what to do
with it

Little Girl

I want to
suck her
age
out
till she is old
till I am young

My Piece

Have her
in pieces
stored
frozen
can
therefore thaw her
anytime
I
want

Enlightenment at the Buddhist Temple

Nine Buddhist monks dead.

The news
says
nothing was taken,
nor was there
any sign
of a
struggle.

Davy's Secret

cthen oI ctouched khis.

RON NYREN

Note

Take beach chair
for sun. If I had
not gone, he had
gone anyway,
it is better I go too.
Pray. Be back God
willing 7–8. Will
treat you my turn.
Stay overnight, we
have to talk.

Put bag please
in the vacuum.

Stories of Your Mouth

You kept landing on the street,
jumping from roofs. I smelled
baby powder and knew you
were there. You tell me
you are my brother, my grandfather.
Or come up to my face and
recite numbers quickly.
Your mouth is larger than my head.
Your mouth pushes me against
a wall, and I jump in.

LESLIE KURTZAHN

Another Dreary Little Poem

It's question-and-answer time
in the forum. It catches us
by surprise. We've all been
sucking on money, fluffing
our cheeks, shifting our loads
to pockets deep in our faces.
Some of us fuss with our underwear.
It seems all of literature has been
a game of The Minister's Cat.
The sounds of construction
were only phantoms echoing
from across the gorge. We have mistaken
whimsy in landscape for information.
We must not be sad. It is such a gas
just to recognize one letter
in the alphabet.

Surplus

Last week's swim, swam, swum. If we could
Only be pluperfect about this! It
Was August, wasn't it, when we thought
The wind blew strongest? Hey, nonny,
Nonny—too many boasts crowding
The harbor bar. Off to sea with us.
We will drown, have our fill of full.
We remember the time that happened before
The time that recently happened. Talk
About undermine—all through high school
We were below sea level, job-sharing with
Trouble. O our mother tongue, we had wanted
To parley you into the sextillion words we
Needed to keep up with last night—to talk
Simply about the about. To give each other
Parole. To sandblast the papyrus.
More to come that hasn't come yet—by which
We mean our own parliament to legislate
The perfect, perfect, perfect, perfect word.

Approaching a City

Dear Mr. Hopper,
              It was just this morning
(why should it seem I have felt all I feel
from the beginning, though I cannot date it,
as though, even before seeing your painting,
even before I knew that I must write you,
I knew whatever I would come to know,
even the manner I would come to know it?)
Mrs. Carmody led us on a tour—
"impartial, though I cannot be expected
not to be human, not have personal favorites"—
through the gallery (light from all directions,
where we would turn, would not yet turn, light spilling
to the paintings themselves, across what Mrs.
Carmody, "though I hesitate to call it
what it requires I call it," calls "the trap
of brutal, obscure corners, corners telling
as much about themselves as about us,
as about Edward Hopper, corners bearing
their secrets almost proudly, if not proudly,
with an uncommon passion," which each canvas
can be said to possess, or be possessed by—
of necessity, Mrs. C would claim—
"corners from which one extricates oneself
not easily or soon, as one would want it,"
the floors, superbly polished, glinting, buffed,
their sheen enough to skate on, each refracting
light pouring from high windows, portholes, fanlights,
halls endlessly turning this way, or that,
endlessly burrowing deeper and deeper
into that maze of vision, complication,

astonishment, awaiting us on walls
ending, just before noon, in a cramped lobby,
a niche, adjacent to a vestibule,
off to one side, easily overlooked
were it not for the nine capital letters,
fittingly emblematic, which the sign bears—
omen? warning? hint of what is to come
in a world where little is known, less given,
where there are damages to be reported?—
nine bold letters in stark relief emblazoned,
stenciled across the lintel: FINAL EXIT)
where, from what seems nothing less
than sheer wisdom,
they have taken it on themselves to hang
that mysterious dreamscape, burdened, haunted,
pinned to its canvas by the unexplained,
to which you have attached the name Approaching
a City, now compelling me to write
in terms you and I shall have understood,
by the end of this letter, not at all,
or at least not enough to make worthwhile
the effort to be put into the reading.
(There are damages here to be reported,
damages which the mind cannot begin
even to weigh, to estimate, to name.)

It is now I must write this, Mr. Hopper,
now I need to begin, before it fades,
dissipates, vanishes, drifts off to smoke
(a fitting image, as becomes apparent),
before whatever sense one shall have made

lies too scattered, too late, at last, to make
what Mrs. Carmody suggests I put down
even if only for that sense of self
unique to each of us, no more, just that,
on behalf of what clarity, what light
it may lend to one's own—her word—"perspective,"
though, of course, it shall not enlarge your own,
you whom these words shall leave just as you were,
unchanged, unmoved, perhaps not moved enough,
at a time you were unaware a student,
changed by your painting, moved more than he knew,
would write to you from ignorance, from need,
from that unholy ground where the two meet.

Before leaving the gallery this morning,
our little tour concluded, one more lesson
in art appreciation at an end
(if not, dear Mrs. Carmody, instruction
in how, at last, to see, or what to live for),
the lobby jammed with other tours and students,
having seen all that they had come to see,
one or two having seen, no doubt, much more,
what, in fact, some had never come to see
(there are damages here to be reported),
arranging us in double matching rows,
apportioned just so, perfectly aligned,
one exactly duplicating the other,
undeviating, orderly, precise,
sightlines pleasing, perspectives shapely, clear,
an artist's eye plotting the whole deployment,
counting to see no one was left behind,

no one dawdled before a favored painting,
lingered admiring shading, angle, scale,
marveling at the quality of brush strokes,
their subtlety, their depth, sheer understatement
trailing off into whispers, evanescence,
at the utter absence of "decoration,"
tonal values wholly in contradiction,
juxtapositions playing off one shade
uncannily against another, each one,
citron, persimmon, lime, mauve, beige, magenta,
unresolved in the background, each small balance
won, for the moment, soon, all too soon, lost,
restive, unquiet, charged, disruptive, drenched
with a drama of unbearable tension
nowhere defined, nowhere definable,
Mrs. Carmody told us we might purchase
a postcard version of that work of art
which spoke most intimately to us, moved us,
moved us deeply, one to a student, even
may have changed us, "though you shall not yet
know that,"
"just to ponder, to study, just to hold to,
later, a moment longer," that one painting
"it may become your joy, even your terror,
those who are the fortunate ones among you,
the ones arriving singularly gifted,
to be unable, as you soon discover—
tomorrow, the day after, a slow learning,
admittedly, an anguish, a climb upward—
utterly unable, to live without."
Most of the others, less fixed from the start

("doomed," perhaps, is the word one might have
     written),
seem to have had some difficulty choosing
which of two or three works they wished to ponder
(study, hold to, live with, attempt to live with),
unlike myself, immediately drawn,
drawn and held, I should tell you, Mr. Hopper,
fatally drawn, perhaps, fatally held,
to the one I am holding here before me
this evening, as I write this, darkness falling,
the one with damages to be reported
beyond the mind to weigh, estimate, name.

It is yours I had chosen, knew I must choose,
yours I ponder, study, begin to live with,
begin, I should say, to attempt to live with
(a long, slow learning, as had been predicted,
more than an anguish, more than a climb upward,
more than anything which might be said of it),
brooding beneath the lamp where I have propped it,
ready, from the evidence, more than ready—
how shall I put this?—to break into flames,
wanting it here before me as I write this,
wanting it haunted, burdened, still amazing,
unforgettable, vivid, unforgotten,
significations spilling from it, omens,
hoping, in time, somehow to make sense of it
(or to make peace with it, which is the same),
even the dimmest, yet not too much sense,
needing to see as fiercely as I can
yet not enough, perhaps, to see too clearly,

that imprecision not quite wholly blind me
to those deeper strangenesses lodged within it.
Knowing neither what my "gifts" are, or may be,
what, tomorrow, I may arrive endowed with
("the ones arriving singularly gifted"),
whether I am, or was, or one day shall be,
for no reason apparent, no just cause,
at risk of turning, slow, dim, unprepared,
inarticulate, seeing not too clearly,
into one of the fabled "fortunate ones,"
I find myself unable, Mr. Hopper,
"utterly unable," to live without
this City of yours, this now mythic City,
ineffable, inevitable, both,
City the maps refuse to chart precisely,
City we make our way to, nameless, placeless,
if not quite back from, darkness falling, fallen
("the trap," she said, "of brutal, obscure corners,"
extrication not simple and not soon,
if at all possible, as you devise it),
you seem, and shall remain forever seeming,
in process (Mrs. C might say "a learning"),
arduous, weighted, long, more than an anguish,
more than a mere climb upward, of Approaching.

I see those rows of windows, row on row,
you wish us to believe comprise a city,
tenements lining some bleak, gutted street
trailing off into twilight's distant suburb,
nothingness, hush, faint whisper, murmur, echo,
the ache of what one knows will not avail,

at the back of the mind, if even there
(shall it be said that others live here, witness
the fall of darkness, evenings, in the dark
tremble, know longing, dream, remember, cry out?),
windows whose curse, whose burden, whose affliction,
unspeakable and eloquent at once,
is, as you have arranged it, Mr. Hopper,
to seem to look not out nor to look in
(when I think of the cost to you, I shudder),
blind windows on a back street nameless, placeless,
in a City—each least detail withheld,
those not withheld magnificently garbled,
those not yet garbled falsified, invented,
those not invented no doubt soon invented,
the map, should there be maps, needing revision,
canceled, revoked, outdated, superseded,
no use whatever to us on a journey
whose hope, whose dream, was to be logical
(no longer the thing hoped for, the thing dreamt),
latitude, season, weather, undisclosed,
our sense of the terrain, geography's
subtleties, certainties, resplendent magic,
lost on us here, late, too late, unredeeming,
outrageously deceptive, fabrications—
it is, it has become, our task, our fate,
to be, without reprieve or intercession,
in however circuitous a fashion
(think of the cost, the toll exacted; shudder),
forever in the process of Approaching—
no more, just that, that alone, mere approach,
not even an advance on, say, the core,

where the City itself lies, the lives in it,
feverish, weathered, glinting, struck, impassioned,
the setting out obscured, the route not straight,
the light too dim, the dark not bright enough,
the damages unspeakable, at best,
more extensive, it happens, than imagined,
destinations unmarked, even if marked
mismarked, misleading, fraudulently promised,
impossible to reach, to reach in time,
to reach where reaching would at last avail,
before the thing to be attained prove wholly
unattainable (how are we to know it
when we arrive there? what small recognition
is to be granted? what hint, what admission,
of vision, omen, flame, signification;
in the end this, this, too: how to pronounce it?
by what name shall it ask that it be called?).

Why should those windows, window after window,
looking not out nor in from blind façades,
overwhelm us with the utterly futile,
the terror of the too symmetrical,
perched high above the cut where tunnel diggers,
hammering day and night, anonymous
(how many seasons, what year, in what weather?),
each with a history unknown to us,
blasted a viaduct that tracks be laid
between the here and there, even approaching
the city, fabled, far, of one's own strangeness?

The thing that breaks the heart, at last, or would,

or soon seems destined to, upon reflection,
will be those murky smudges splayed on concrete,
overhead, where the train enters the tunnel
(where, at least, one assumes trains enter tunnels),
arriving and departing every evening
as trains never have and yet always shall,
keeping quite scrupulously to a schedule
obsolete by the time one seeks connections—
for just how many years is it now, tell me;
one loses count, needs, of course, to lose count—
several mud-brown brush strokes artfully
arranged not to seem artfully arranged,
little soot marks smoke has left where the engine
slows on the downgrade near the viaduct
(all progress, any progress, being progress
into the tracklessness of one's own strangeness),
their true color bled from them, toneless, muted
to the brink of imminent disappearance
(a small detail, admittedly, yet one
so touched with grace, with anguish, so unasked-for,
so contained in the cry it would cry out,
so consistent with the vision presented,
so much a piece with the rest, with the silence
welling from windows, tenements, with tunnels
waiting for trains one knows will never come,
never keep quite scrupulously to schedule,
with namelessness, with placelessness, with darkness
forever falling here, never quite fallen
("corners bearing their secrets almost proudly"),
one shall not search beyond it for, say, "meaning"—
no need to ask the artist what he "meant,"

Mrs. C tells us; "he is last to know")—
nearly an inadvertence on your part,
it would seem, Mr. Hopper, but not quite,
painted as flat, as dry, as unobtrusive
as paint and brush and thinner hope to make them,
discoloration, living stain, the mark
of weather having come and having gone,
passing through suburbs resolutely nameless,
leaving us as we were, as we shall be,
weatherless, timeless, parched, in a dry season
knowing no year, no border, no reprieve,
pale smoke of engines rising as the railbed
leads the train deeper, deeper, underground
and the view closes in on implication,
where all trace of the local, the express,
the in-betweens long since dropped from the schedule,
once passing here, once stopping, once departing,
once partaking of all that trains partook,
clamor, fever, passion of embarkation,
will have been quite effectively erased,
obliterated, turned, in fact, to smoke—

a little thing, perhaps, a final stroke,
coda, footnote, finishing touch, summation,
minor and wayward, random, fragmentary,
not meant to be more than last-minute, yet
crucial to vision, to what one would see,
delicate and detailed, caring enough,
even meticulous enough, to wrench us
back to the look of the approach, the look
of suburbs which lead, must lead, either way—

into, out of, neither, both—the look
of whatever burns itself in the mind
and stays, retained, contained, held long,
held fiercely,
all things tenuous, late, beleaguered, scorched,
intended to be no more than passed over
in a glance, in a word ("appreciation,"
museum tours, lessons in how to see,
in what, at last, to live for, unavailing,
despite your efforts, Mrs. C), the look,
even, of approaching a city for which
there is no name, there never was a name
(all names proving, in the end, dispossessions),
there may not even have been an approach
(there are damages here to be reported,
Mrs. Carmody might have warned, but failed to),
yet a city we seem destined to know,
know at once (the fortunate ones among us,
those of us marked as singularly gifted),
one it seems our fate is not to mistake,
even in a failed season such as this,
misjudge the nature of, the distance to,
however bleak, ungainly, slow, our progress
in reaching some accommodation with it,
not see clearly (though, in conformity
with those principles earlier established,
one might wish not too clearly, Mr. Hopper),
nor understand the vein of desolation
from which the stones that pave these streets are
      mined,
that front the blind façades above the cut

where, downgrade, downgrade, trains take to the
    tunnel
as they always have and yet never shall,
where each of us grows now a little darker
in the evening, beneath the viaduct
(there are damages here still unreported),
discoloration, weather mark, time stain,
and the heart comes to know, at last, what breaks it.

                                        for Lynda Hull

The Market on La Cienega

Before they go to work, the butchers
sterilize their hands. Still,
they are unclean. I watch
the butcher named Tomas pretend
a pig is giving him a blowjob.
Holding its face to his crotch, he
dances among the metal tables
stacked with meat.

In another life, the early sun
warming the back of its head, the pig
stretches its legs
and tries to remember the dream
it just woke up from.

Crackle

Her mind hurts at the corners
As if someone has twisted each end,
Two knots holding the sheath
Over a piece of candy.
Don't touch the silvery foil.

Last night, in a dream,
She thought of what the doctor said
Before he removed the lump.
You could dance naked on a table,
And no one would see.
When she woke up,
She touched the spot.
There was a dent,
Like a smile.

She knows a woman
Who has a row of wigs,
Who at night sleeps bald.

The crackly paper shifts
As she turns to look outside.
She remembers now
The way she felt as a child, stepping,
Wading, in a prim expanse
Of lace and dead leaves.

The Ordinary World

It was not his story,
And yet there he was with his ax,
Chopping his way in.
Dazed, we jumped out,
Already unused to sunlight
And the ordinary world.

The Wolf slept on,
Smiling in his dreams
About the women in his belly.

Being eaten?
It was exciting.
He took me in one red swallow.

Now life is the path
From Mother's to Grandmother's,
And the Wolf, God help me, is dead.

The Hinge

Those years everything seemed
To be about wings—feathers
I lifted from the cool grass;
Junior pilot's wings
My father brought home
With hotel soap and the wrung look
He wore as the airplane
Released him from its pressurized mouth;
Ribbons that dangled satiny and slim
From my bedpost
While at night I dreamt of doves.
At Sunday school they meant forgiveness.
But, in the dark tower of sleep,
I held them; I wanted to find the hinge
That divided those creatures
From the rest of us.

I never found the hinge,
And I don't remember when I stopped looking.
One day, sitting in the late afternoon shade
With bits of light scrabbling through it,
I thought briefly about the wings.
Maybe the light opened up for a moment
And I saw doves. Then shadows.
Applause lies sealed away with ribbons
In a manila envelope.
Sleep clicks each day shut
Like a purse, all its prisoners
Wadded up into darkness.

Summit

Standing on
the bridge above dawn,
I have a sack of adjectives on my shoulder.

I could have been a dangerous man.
I could have been a better man.
Only the fish look up.

Jeptha Lake

I strapped on my blades and drove my blood
into wind, until the hollowed-out
hull of me filled with lightning.
I skated backwards, pulling the town
out through the lights in its windows;
skated until the brown-haired girl
along the bank vanished.
The paper mill flew off.
The train went by on its blades.
All the wind that ever was.
And I never knew so much of life
was dancing.

Flying

Neighbors slant
for their cars
from homes welded at the hip.
They have forgotten to look
out wherever their elbows point,
to smash the time clocks that hang
inside them, round as a face.
I slam across our lawn until that
yellow smacker is up there and flying,
come out between two buildings
with a paper cup in my teeth.
Two couples on their slab of walkway,
their legs in the grass.
More tires on road gravel.
Eyes throwing themselves through car roofs.
Then night. Pulling the moth in.
Pulling the gold moth right through me.

Fight

I take one in the gut,
crawl to the curb and puke
into the lap of the
guy who counts
blows.

I hit this mother-
fucker, this dinosaur, hit-
hit, until I taste
the rib-split, the Jell-O,
his eyes rolling back
into rosary beads.

Bout after,
I drink down names
in my mouth, animal sounds,

find this coon
with its tongue
on pause, lapping up
its own blood.

Curl around it.
Heart. Fur. Sleep.

The Reading

I want riderless tractors idling up to this tower,
pickup trucks with CB antennas. I want trees to sprout
through the pavement each time a poet takes a step,
Elm trees with white-winged angels in them,
Elm trees with crows and apples, with children
swinging from ropes. I want a billboard of me lit up
by a helicopter, traffic backed up
in one long tongue of metal. People will climb to
their car roofs as I rappel down to my reading,
shoving my fist through that billboard,
knocking my own teeth out. When you walk from your
        car,
magazines will fly up to you, slap you in the face.
People will go around mummified by poetry.
When the doors to this tower open, everyone will
be sucked in on one great breath.
Whales will be heard in the train yards.
Young ones will cup their hands to their parents' ears
to whisper my secrets. At some point my poison
ivy will boil open. Demons will flare out of me,
broil and hiss, smacking their wings against walls,
lampshades, faces. You will feel yourself breathing,
will see fingerprints you have left on other people's
bodies, see feathers smoking on walls. The elevator will
rattle up and down its black throat until it opens,
until my
twin steps out, climbs into this body, finds my
mouth with
his mouth. You will grab yourself by your clothes
and snap them out over this room with you still in
        them.

You will come to and say nothing.
My old man will get up and leave, start a crap game
on the elevator with my brothers Joe Dietz,
Leo Tosoian, Joe Pellerito, and the other scrub boys
from Detroit. They will blow into their hands, rattle
the dice until the spots come off the spotted dress.
And I'll be gone with them, my body still propped up
before you, some long hand in me moving my mouth
as the elevator opens its accordion doors on each floor.
Wherever you are in you, I want to wake you up,
find a gold horn in your bones,
and blow a fine blue spread right through you.
When you tap at the floor to keep time,
faraway fruit will club the ground
beneath trees and roll off into this city,
skipping up porches, raining
into the back seats of convertibles,
rolling up the curve of a squirrel's back.
Today, I want to lay out the Detroit River
with a gold-hulled freighter on it,
lay out that street I grew up on,
lay it out in the space between one clock tick,
show you Greg Grillo pumping his arms
around the corner at Siminely's, his fists jabbing
with the stopwatch in his old-man's hand.
I want to spit a tooth out at you, jab you in the cheek,
a Rybicki scar for you to walk around with.
I want my grandma's dust to blow up
on this tenth-floor ledge, for her to materialize
in front of us, Marjorie Wallace, a little girl
in Ottawa

with ice skates over her shoulder, waving to us
to step out over the ledge and skate. One vision
laid out
between each clock tick. The moon pacing its light by
us.
The earth rocking, rocking ever so slowly.

In the Can After Work:
Letter to Hutch

Hutch, too much smoke is blowing
along the space between us. We can barely see
each other flying from the backs of two great birds.
Remember that dust-bowl ghost,
town in the Huron Mountains
where we whacked knuckle-sized deer flies
off each other, dropping our mouths
into our Chunky Soup? Brother,
my insides can still split
a great Red Sea for us to walk between,
tilted pots at our feet, musky heads;
a wall of water in a Spielberg dream:
time clocks floating in it, guitar strings,
the confetti that we saw falling
on our walks through the forest.
When you buffed one of my old man's cars,
the whole chassis rocked.
When you laid your hands against wood,
root music broke into your throat.
This morning I thought my body had gone too far
into the bass bottom of the cornfield.
I tossed these pills back
into the wishing well,
spun a couple of hundred thousand lug nuts
on and off my fingers, lifted this
onto the half-box fridge in the can at work.
These country Joes kept coming in,
laughing, a blue-wax blend
of soap and grease on their hands.
I lifted this machine up,
watched their mouths go chasing

back into the shop after their Budweiser cans.
I can see us laughing in white bubbles,
kicking our legs through the cold blue
waters of Georgian Bay; can see me punching
the gas and brakes to dodge your bullet snowballs;
or watching you scale the side of a building
that dawn after your first guitar was christened
Karen. Only getting to a spec of it,
casting this silver lure in a moon arc,
slipping down into the Great Northwest.

Pastorale

Who goes to meet the carriage
Stumbles, climbing in.
There is no snow in Eden,
But chew the bitter wind.

Stop Talking About Writing

I'm talking about the hairpin of activity. What you pull out in a state of lethargy, when siblings have become surgeons, bankers, engineers, and your choice has been that of an explorer. Your choice has been that of an explorer, an ignorer of securities tied up in the neat knot of shoelaces, a looker and a loser of nothing. I'm talking about unattachments.

As I looked for a timely diversion and took several suggestions from the most important person, squirming eased the zipper and I poked my matted head through the slit slowly opening in the coin purse. I was getting away from money, crawling through the coin slot, shoving the stamps back up into the vending machine from which they come, which can be tricky. You have to wait for the right moment, when no one's looking but everyone's paying attention. You can do it any day, but after-hours or Saturdays are the best.

It's a cyclical thing that comes back every few weeks, like a good casserole you're willing to put the time and ingredients into. It's a desire to be prolific but not wanting to force it. There's terrific pain in rupture and in the moment of pleasure, the moment when it comes out just the way you want it, when your meaning is eloquently expressed, when it becomes like talking, but you've stopped all that.

Reeling

The secret lies not in the kite but in the string.
The kite behaves—wind gives it loft,
The calm declination—it
Knows its physics.
No magic there.
But the string is another story.
Serves both masters, that.
Trails away, bows, makes the connection.
Spools off obedient as a gun dog.
No complications, until later,
You retrieve the kite, thinking
This is the quarry,
And pull in snarls set in air,
Butterflies of twine.

On Vacation

My muse and I swim together
In a motel pool off Highway 85.
She wears a one-piece suit
And sidestrokes easily,
While I lunge ahead with choppy pulls,
Open to the sea.

The water is squared off,
Confined to a perfect geometry.
She urges me to
Swim every day, do sprints,
Practice holding my breath under water.
I finish a lap, gasping, hoist myself out.
Old men use the stairs.
I look for her to go back to the room.
She is talking with a couple from Garden City,
Kansas, who are crossing the country
With their children.

The Man Crossing Stout

I watched a man cross Stout Street yesterday.
He left a car by the curb and
Walked as if entering the sea.
The tide of traffic rushed by him,
A wreck of blue suit with pencil stripe
And pressed pocket linen. Foundering,
His shoulders sagged, his face was set.
What terrible news did he carry?
Had some hand separated his ribs and
Touched the round, slick stone that was his heart?
He drifted to the far side and there,
Finding one of its star points, pulled the handkerchief,
Already moist, from his jacket and sponged
His salt-white face. He moved off,
Carrying his sadness like ballast
Deep in the hold.

Thermodynamics

Darling,
In answer to your question:

$$dS°rxn = [S°(us)] - [S°(you) + S°(me)] = 245.3 \, J/K$$

or,
As more eloquently articulated by Yeats,
Things fall apart.

PATRICK EHLEN

Estranged Wife Slams Fist Down on Husband's Keyboard

ujuuuuuuuuyik

Dear Sir

At issue here in our last meeting the reluctance of a strong bargaining position to decide upon and therefore regrettably of course in response to however the matter in question ipso facto and conceivably indeed to the tune of sound mind and body of knowledge

in fact your interpretation in other words hereby releases all claims in accordance with the terms of said contradictory evidence for the record as per our agreement

Sincerely,

Early Mass

Because his father was a fisherman,
part of the Gortons' fleet out of Gloucester,
the pastor said early mass himself. He
stood at the unlit door of the chapel,
cold meeting cold, to greet
his brethren, the fish-sellers of our town,
who had an hour or so before they
returned to their red-washed wharf huts to grade
the iridescent catch.
Oh, some fishermen came too, drunk or hung
up in dry dock, and the pastor would close
the rain-blown doors, happy before the new
tabernacle of God in his own house.

Because he sat all night monitoring
the stations of the shortwave radio,
my father went to early mass and I
went too, perched with him in the back row near
the old Portuguese men who shivered in
their open-work vests, their jackets sharp from
brushing.

Sometimes my father smelt of rye, of all
night in the same chair. But more often my
father smelled of steam, of bathwater, of
towels. He was so clean. The morning grew
outside the chill safety of that codfish
church. We begin again with nothing to
fear but sadness.

I Tell Her Slower

:
the way she would
if she were doing this
to God.

To His Holiness

Listen, my birthday's coming up.
Maybe you could send me
a real beeswax marvel, like the one
they light every Easter, a flowing
Lawrence-of-Arabia robe, a couple
of those cardinal-red sashes.
Perhaps you could even throw in
a miter and Eagle.
And how about a pair of those
papal-blue slippers with the gold
crisscrossed keys of Heaven
embroidered on the vamps.
By the way—and don't take offense—
but you guys lost me
when you turned palsy-walsy.

Family Pictures

Rose loved Morris
terribly.
Morris loved Rose
among others.
They spoiled the baby.
Money was easy.
Time wasn't.

Long Distance to an Aging Father

Today we talk about the price of plums.
The black ones he just bought
for fifty-nine cents a pound.
"Big as doorknobs," he tells me.
"And juicy."
Wants me to hold
so he can wash his hands.

One Day

I'll wake up
and find myself
on the six o'clock news
after having stabbed you
over some little thing
that happened once too often
and to which
I may have overreacted.

Monkey Back

It is a hard lump, and a perfect circle. It could be an extra nub of vertebra at the base of his neck, an unnamed protrusion. The flesh is different, feels patchy, the pores closed over. It is whiter than the rest of him. It moves along with him. He keeps vowing to get the thing cut off. But I do not want him to do it. I bit it once. There was no blood. He did not cry out. When he is sleeping beneath me, I touch it, feel this pale knot in the palm of my yellow hand. I could take it anytime. I could slit the skin with his ebony letter opener. I could lift it out. I could slide off him, slip away with it, back to where I came from.

Granatelli Refutes the Buddha

Sorry, Lord of Light, it's not
the journey but the being
there, just under the flags, *then*.

The entire universe in
my rearview, scenery the
obstacle overcome.

Generation

I wonder how it felt:
his rough hands, stained with ink and grease,
                    as he braced me
            against the sink and brushed

            my pink skin with soapy
water; and what difference from
                    hers, already
            wrinkled at the tips from the girls'

            permanents, or washing
woolens and hose in the bathroom.
                    Which, I wonder,
            did I prefer? Whom, out

of all time, would I select now?

1965

We were only playing doctor—
feeling one thing move, another
                    not. Then
            everything was wet, and I

breathed as though I had run the whole
length of the playground to capture
                    her, chain
            torn apart, Red Rover.

            The clouds were like windows.
I covered myself with her hair.

Brad and Mary Jo at the Park

Stand up, the little boy cries, *stand
        up*. And the baby in
        the walker pushes her
bootied toes against the concrete,

and Mommy says, *Good girl, good girl,*
        and Daddy turns the page
        of his magazine with
one damp finger. *Cocorico,*

chirps the bird on the branch, *ma 'tite
        fille*. Because it's spring.
        Because the sun spins on
its tether in the sky. Because

        I love you.

Logistical

Whenever
I find myself on the top,
someone I love shudders
on the bottom.

The Other Lives of Trains

He rode facing east all the way across the continent.
His face accompanied him there on the window to his
    side,

at night occasionally pierced by lights
from farms in the distance or passing cars.

Once for many miles one ran parallel,
its headlights streaking along in his jugular vein.

Beauty Alone Has No Edge

A series of objects that lends
A series of

Along the windowsill lined up
These artifacts:

Did you return?
Yes, yes, it had no boundary

And the six-fingered child
The intricate musical instruments

We living again go on in the
Yes, yes, the inseparable colors

The present world would
A series of objects that could have

Dark against the sky
A perfect line

No, not migrating geese, you said
At first and then, just

Because it was simpler, lied.

The Occupation

The soldiers have come and gone in waves not fit to ride and now our house is stalled. I walk the streets and from bad angles see their tanks jerk by, the drivers snickering as my guns gather dust on the garage shelves. "They didn't take everything, did they?" my wife says. She wears a dress stitched from a tablecloth. Soon we will have a child who will call me Ulysses. "No," I say, "they left the begonias." And they did. And they are waxy and creep. And tilt against the defeated lawn.

1. WHY DID YOU DO IT?

He wants to be famous indoors. He wants to be the most famous there ever was indoors. He wants people to walk up to him indoors and rub into his famous, to say they touched it.

2. WHERE DID YOU GET THE IDEA?

He thinks that he takes too many pills. He thinks the rest of us take too many pills. He takes pills for his emotions. He takes a pill to remember to take his pills.

3. DID YOU HAVE ANYONE HELP YOU?

He mentioned something to a woman in a bar. He showed her his tongue. He showed her the pill he was taking. She asked for one and swallowed it. She looked him in the eye for two hours.

4. WHEN DID YOU FIRST MEET HER? HOW LONG WAS THE MEETING?

He wants to buy a watch that tells time miles below the surface of the ocean, a watch that works even if tanks roll over it, a watch you can take with you to the farthest regions of space, a watch that works at the edge of time, a watch that brings time to those parts of the universe where there is no time. He thinks a watch like this could make you very happy. He would like to find a watch like this.

5. COULD YOU ANSWER THAT AGAIN?

It would be impulsive to buy a watch like that.

6. DID SHE PROMISE YOU ANYTHING? DID SHE HINT AT ANYTHING?

He would like to be falsely accused of something so he could deny it. He would like the resulting publicity to suggest that he was guilty. Then he would like a second wave of publicity to suggest that he was not guilty of that but was guilty of something else, something deeper, guilty of no crime that could be punished.

7. THE IMPLICATION WAS THAT YOU WOULD DO IT IN THE BEDROOM. IS THAT WHAT SHE PROMISED YOU?

He has been told that he is not as famous as he should be. To be famous, you have to be famous. If you're not famous, you'll never be famous. He wonders how he can be famous indoors.

8. How many times did you do it? Did she say she liked it?

He remembers what he said one night to the committee: "You can't discard me. I'm not one of your discardables." He remembers them looking at him with amazement. He remembers them saying, "Who is he?" and then, "Who was he?" They never said, "Who will he be?"

9. What happened when you took it out?

He wants to wear an underwater watchband deep in the ocean, at the bottom of the Marianas Trench, where the fish are iridescent green and blue and have their tongues cut out.

10. Did she understand what she was doing?

He thinks it will be easier once he learns to concentrate. He thinks it will be possible once he learns to concentrate. There is a trick to it.

11. What do you think?

He has no basis for this thought.

12. What happened when the police came?

He was alarmed, confused, excited, ashamed, joyful, eager to please, capriciously cruel, playfully ignorant.

13. Do you like to clean up?

It makes him feel good.

14. Did she seem threatening?

He thinks that no one else is concerned about being fair. He feels we all walk around not knowing why we are cheated, not knowing this is the cause of being cheated.

15. Was that when you had the first attack?

Suppose this. Suppose you are standing on the street corner immersed in self-pity. Will you see anyone come up and offer to join you?

16. WHAT DID YOU THINK OF HER AFTERWARD?
He can't put his finger on it. Dogs have it easier.

17. WOULD YOU DO IT AGAIN?
The fear of being turned down by voluptuous women haunts him. At times he imagines them on the sofa.

18. DID YOU GET PHYSICAL?
Let me say this.

19. DID IT GET ALL OVER HER?
See, he could be talking all the time. He thinks he doesn't want to give that up. He thinks that anything you do, don't you do?

20. DO THESE QUESTIONS BOTHER YOU?
Look.

21. HAVE YOU THOUGHT ABOUT THE TRIAL?
The defense of the righteous, the unruly, the truly incompatible.

22. DO YOU SLEEP WELL AT NIGHT?
He will lose his friends, the people who were posing as his friends but who, in fact, in reality, were just waiting for something spectacular like this so they would no longer have to pretend to be his friends.

23. THEY MIGHT HAVE UNDERSTOOD IF YOU HAD DONE IT ONCE.
He thinks it may have happened when he was blinking his eyes at fifteen frames a second.

24. WHY DID YOU SHOW NO REMORSE?
He thinks they take pity on him for this. He wonders why they never tell him they are taking pity on him. It is because they take pity on him.

25. EH?
This is an unruly way of being. This is not being there.

26. IS THERE ANYTHING ELSE YOU WANT TO SAY?
Some things you can't explain. **Q**

Please, folks, let me through - I'm a meteorologist.

Heathcliff makes lasagna

I get all the news from Blackwater as Mamie writes me and Sunny calls me, etc., etc. Mamie writes that she has some buyers for her house, but now Sunny says in a phone call that that fell through. Mamie wants to move because she can't stand living alone, but Sunny and I and the rest of the family don't want her to move. We want Mamie to stay right there and provide a place for us in Blackwater, to be the Old Home Place, to be like The Mother. Or like The Grandmother. You know. Where we can go and stay out in the beauty shop and be close to Mama's house, which was Great-Grandpa Albert Racy's house, and the next-door neighbor is harvesting his garden tobacco like he does every year and hanging it up to dry and shooting dice with The Girls and so on. We are hoping nobody buys it. And the other thing is, damn you, how come you always have to put the Blackwater letters right next to a nasty picture?!! I want to send these things to Mamie and The Girls, and they're all good Baptists and First Christian Church people that shoot dice and keep possums, and here are all these dirty pitchers of cunts and dorks and people poking one another without surcease and spreading diseases. It is just too raucous to send to Mamie, and she would leave it lying around the house for Mildred Cornine to find—who is not a member of The Girls. My God, Mildred has already taken her piano out of the church over some dispute with Mamie. God knows what would happen if this outrage of yours were to be discovered. Letters about Mamie right next to Degrading Pornographic Material! This is no joke. There are consequences. Mamie said in her letter that Archie Cornine passed away. She said, "All us cousins are about gone." First cousins are really an important group. Well, back in the old days they were. There's a word for it in Zulu, anyway. It was important in settled rural communities. There were the twins, Bea and Bo, and R. D. Landon, who once dressed up in a dress and a wig and went around Blackwater trying to sell Avon, and Miss Priss Mildred Cornine, who was always Taking Umbrage, and Wib and Walter Racy, who used to go around in a pickup smashing down highway signs. Why don't sociologists bother with these things? Why are they always off studying Urdu "kinship relations"? Jim and I went to the 21st Annual Chilympiad, the Chili Cook-Off in San Marcos. It was very crowded with chili stands and competitors, contests, boots, hats, and outrageousness. The chili-cooking teams had set up booths; everybody had to cook over a woodfire or a Coleman. There were Arkansas and Louisiana teams and people from all over Texas. Everybody was to offer samples—but by the time we got there, nothing was left. The names they gave their concoctions leaned toward the Satanic: The Dharma Burns, Boneyard Red, Butt-Burner, The Devil's Own, Hellfire Jalapeño, and Hell-Bitch Red. A section was partitioned off for the judges, and they all sat there, older men and women in bright red vests, tasting. Beer and crackers were being passed around. Jim and I stood in front of the grandstand to watch; the announcer announced that there was now to be a belt-buckle contest; and with a little urging, some people would slowly walk up onstage with this kind of aw-shucks shuffle; the announcer said, "Hey, some of you are going to have to suck it in before we can see 'em." There was a dance band and cowboys dancing. You can always tell a real cowboy on the dance floor because they are always completely incapable of dancing but always drunk enough to try and are always shifting stiffly around in a grim, formal pace and attempting to stand upright. All the chili stands also had bottles lined up in front. I couldn't figure it out, but it seemed to be some kind of custom. By Saturday evening each stand had empty Boone's Farm wine bottles, rye whiskey, tequila, and scotch bottles in a triumphant line, like, "Hey, we *drank* all this!" We scrounged some more for chili, but it was still all gone. I saw a man walk past that had on a T-shirt that said something about Save The Rivers—a piece of legible clothing with an ecology message. I was struck by how out-of-place the man was, how instantly identifiable as a type. Just the message on the T-shirt. Save The Rivers is pretty different from Try My Hell-Bitch Red. To tell you the truth, I don't like the joylessness of T-shirts with morally instructive *commands* on them. There is something of Mildred Cornine in it. Is it a defect in my nature? Anyway, I would save a river if I could, but I won't be ordered around, especially not by a T-shirt. Gripe, gripe. Only, in looking for some books on Vietnamese culture and history at the library the other day, I came upon Mary McCarthy's *Hanoi*, and just could not believe what I was reading. Thus it is with folks like myself who become incensed and must stand up and denounce and do nothing but make fools of themselves. **Q**

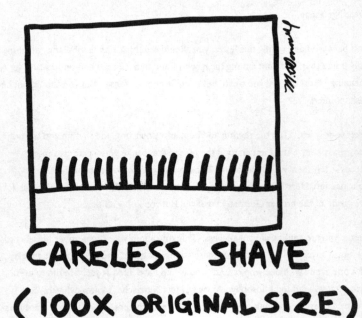

CARELESS SHAVE
(100X ORIGINAL SIZE)

October 15

Dear Nietzsche,

Just because I am writing this letter, you should not think I am a scholar or anything vulgar like that. I am not among those who claim to have read and understood your meaning. Most of what you wrote never made enough sense. But you should not be disappointed.

I felt your spirit. I felt the rhythm and beat in your writing, the rhythm and beat of the great poem. And I understood the reason that broke your sentences into pieces — left them all hyphenated. Those sentences could not bear the weight of your passion, Herr Nietzsche, that is why they shattered. It was simply too much for the girdle of the proper German language. But you know all that.

I hope you are smiling at your success. Thinking about you, I remember these words by James Joyce: "When one reads these strange pages of one long gone one feels that one is one with one who once..." You would have liked Joyce. He did to literature what you did to philosophy. Anyway, Herr Nietzsche, I know what Joyce means. Everytime I think of you, there you are, in the present, with your giant mustache and gleaming forehead full of philosophy. You are the dream on fire, spewing words of the poetry misunderstood. How could I not write you this letter?

Besides, today is such a special day. Happy birthday, Herr Nietzsche!

Ihr ergebene,

Shahid Hoda

I

In the park, people were reading, looking up at the sun. The ground shook. A hand stuck up, a head. People went running, screaming. The head was blond, blue-eyed. It was smiling. Am I in Soho? it said. Park guys came. They pushed the head down, banged it with a shovel, buried it. They moved a bench over the spot. "There," they said, "you shouldn't have any more trouble."

II

There was a squeaking in his chest. Dave jumped up. "I'm having a heart attack!" He rushed to a doctor. The doctor listened to his heart. He heard talking. "You swallow a transistor? Wait," he said, "it's God. God is talking in you. He says he is very busy. Lots of sparrows fall, he doesn't notice. Guys bless themselves, miss baskets, get knocked out. There are too many lotteries. He needs a deputy. You, Dave. Would he do that?" Dave nodded and went about his business.

III

The supervisor came out of his office. "There is no meaning to life," he said. "It is pointless, right?" No one answered. He shrugged, opened the window and jumped. His secretary followed. "He's never been wrong yet," she said. The guy sweeping the hall threw down his broom. "Might be fun," he said, "this isn't." Next, an accountant who said he was too honest, a lawyer who wrote poetry. Two security guys came running. They boarded up the window, looked around, and left.

IV

She banged on his door at three in the morning. He didn't know her. "In," she said, "let me in." He did. "Let me see," she said, "I want to see." She opened his closets, tossed stuff on the floor, read his diary. "Let me do it," she said, pushing him onto the bed. She straddled him, screaming. "This is all?" she said. He nodded. "Out!" she said. "Let me out."

V

Della and Mike were having breakfast, reading the paper. There was shouting in the street. Della went to the window. Indians were riding up and down, chasing people, shooting flaming arrows. Traffic was stopped. The newsstand was in flames. An arrow came in the window. Della screamed, stamping it out. Mike took off his glasses. "What the hell is going on?" he said. He went to the window. He said, "Yo, Native Americans! Ride west ten blocks! Take the IRT at the corner to White Plains!" An Indian in a long headdress raised his hand. They rode off.

VI

I was old, fifty. I had gray in my beard, bags under my eyes. I was going to die. Mona came up to me. I was in love with her. She kissed me, unbuttoned her blouse. "Arnie," she said, "my gift to you." Oh, Lord. My buddy's wife took me aside. "Finally you're handsome," she whispered. "I'm yours." "Such a patina," my analyst said, "what hotel?" Her secretary wrote me a note. I was so wise, she would do anything. I drove out to see my old man. He had this big house in the suburbs. He was on the patio, wearing an ascot, a cigar stuck in his face. "You son-of-a-bitch," I said, "you never told me."

VII

The visual culture is at hand. The image dominates. The word is hard. It resists. Film and television control. There is no psychological depth. There is no perspective. There is no patience. There is no history. Everything is accomplished now. Now is eternity. Pleasure is now. Denial is unbearable. All things are new. We are bored. We are volatile. The unspeakable happens. There are no consequences. Attention is curt. Words must be few. **Q**

NORMAN MAILER'S NEW THEORY OF
PERSONALITY: "EVERY BANANA
IS DIVIDED INTO TWO COMPLETE
AND DIFFERENT BANANAS."

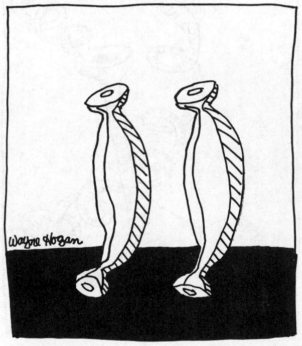

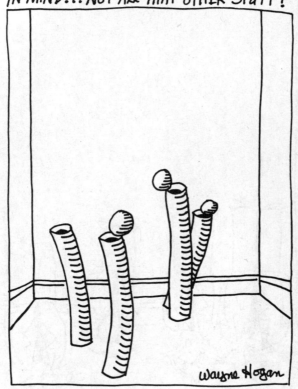

NEW WAY TO SLEEP

GOOD BOOTS, HONEST BOOTS, TRUE BOOTS

RECENT RECIPIENT OF $335,000
MACARTHUR AWARD FOR HIS CRITICALLY
ACCLAIMED WORK AS DECADE'S
FLASHIEST DRESSER ON A STOOL

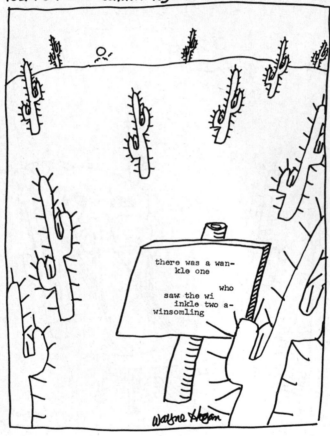

ANALYSIS IS ONE THING; REALITY IS ANOTHER

NOTES OF THE GREATEST LIVING WRITER—
TUESDAY, CLOUDY AND WARM

There has so far been one basic reaction to my work: none. No sooner do I release my most heartfelt tale than a post-nuclear silence falls over the city. By my few readers I am misunderstood. Forced to read my work, they ask: Where will the story ever begin? When will you stop chattering, complaining, and explaining long enough for some action to take place? And here is the rub. I dress like my contemporaries and live beside them, yet my soul is that of some great long-dead Russian poet. I sit still and listen to the wind of eternity while others eat TV. I am the greatest living writer.

What's wrong?
I am often asked this question as I run along at my top speed, gasping, apoplectic. It is so difficult to write when you are running. The pen dances and skitters over the page. If I use all my will to control my script, it becomes crabbed and painful, unreadable. Also, one looks down and before he knows it, he's flipped over a hydrant or nearly split himself lengthwise against a pole.

Why are you always running? my friends call out as I pass in a blur. They drive up alongside me and try to entice me into their cars. They imply with delicacy that I am in need of professional care.

Fuck off! I gasp.

Yet they remain my friends and admirers. I am, to them, a sort of hero, a symbol. Of what, I do not know, but there is something in the way they wag their heads sadly that makes me know I am at once an object of veneration and derision.

When I tell them to fuck off, their awe increases. Who tells people to fuck off?

I became a writer because my mother wanted me to. She decided to create a writer. She was a very beautiful woman. While my father was on the road selling neckties, she seduced a certain Nobel Laureate from Poland and gave birth, without Father's knowledge, to me. I met my real father only once. He was lecturing at the University of Chicago. Upon learning I was his son, he took my hand, shook it, and said, "Hello, so good to meet you. And now I'm going to get some fish." He walked to the food table and was immediately swarmed over by people wanting to stick their fingers in his brain and up his ass.

My mother shut me up in a room with all sorts of great works and a pile of paper beside a typewriter. By my fifteenth birthday I had begun a mammoth novel entitled *A Young Man's Journey*. For fifteen hundred pages, I discussed my first day of school. The book was never finished as I forgot what I had for lunch. It might have been tuna, might have been bologna. It might have been anything.

I'll tell you what. Everyone in the whole world has decided to be the world's greatest writer.

How depressing it is. How dreadful that we have changed from a world of readers to a world of scribblers, scritching and scratching, processing and typing to be heard.

I sit at my corner table in the café. Around me people gab about plot and character. Denouement. (Have I spelled it correctly? If so, what does it mean?) Pathos and bathos. Advances. Were I to put a pistol in my mouth and spray the wall with my brains, they would all rush to their rooms to write about it. First, some would step close to touch the wall and lick their finger, just to know if the spectacle was real.

Time to run. **Q**

For credit-card orders of back numbers, call toll-free, at 1-800-733-3000. Prices and isbn codes shown below. Or purchase by check or money order via letter to Subscription Office. Note addition of postage and handling charge at $1.50 the copy per each copy requested.

Q1	$6.95	394-74697-x	Q12	$7.95	679-72153-3
Q2	$5.95	394-74698-8	Q13	$8.95	679-72743-4
Q3	$5.95	394-75536-7	Q14	$8.95	679-72893-7
Q4	$5.95	394-75537-5	Q15	$9.95	679-73231-4
Q5	$6.95	394-75718-1	Q16	$9.95	679-73244-6
Q6	$6.95	394-75719-x	Q17	$10.00	679-73494-5
Q7	$6.95	394-75936-2	Q18	$10.00	679-73495-3
Q8	$6.95	394-75937-0	Q19	$10.00	679-73690-5
Q9	$7.95	679-72139-8	Q20	$10.00	679-73691-3
Q10	$7.95	679-72172-x	Q21	$10.00	679-73862-2
Q11	$7.95	679-72173-8	Q22	$12.00	679-74050-3